FREE AS A BIRD

TO Rachel
with warmest best wishes
on Sun, 30th - August 98 — *Prain — De*
Rochia
Feel free As A Bird Rachel
Reading this Book —.

FREE AS
A BIRD

Same - To Rachel
Patrick Touher .

Patrick Touher

GILL & MACMILLAN

Published in Ireland by
Gill & Macmillan Ltd
Goldenbridge
Dublin 8
with associated companies throughout the world

© Patrick Touher 1994
0 7171 2176 3

Designed by Fergus O'Keeffe
Print origination by O'K Graphic Design, Dublin

Printed by
ColourBooks Ltd, Dublin

A catalogue record for this book is available from the British Library.

5 4 3 2 1

I dedicate this book to my wife, Pauline, who has stood by me in times of utter despair, and to our happy children, Paula, John, and Suzanne Maria.

Contents

Acknowledgments	ix
Prologue	1
Free as a Bird	9
Buttermilk and Apple Pie	20
Home Again	29
What an Explosion!	38
My First Date	44
The Isle of Man	51
Liverpool and London	57
The Pawnshop	68
Itchy Feet	73
St Brelade's Bay	80
A Picture of You	88
Near Death Do I Sleep	99
Bradford Royal	105
The Shadow of Artane	112
Bon Voyage	119
Strange Customs	131
A Face from the Past	147
The Overlander	153
The Ballroom of Romance	164
A Home of My Own	171
Love and Marriage	179
Inspired to Write	188
Conclusion	195

Acknowledgments

My grateful thanks to journalist Liz Ryan, *Evening Herald*, for encouraging me and for telling me I can write.

To the staff of the *Fingal and Drogheda Independent* for showing such a keen interest in me and for the smashing photographs.

I wish to thank Niamh for her hard work in typing my handwritten script for this book and the staff of the Balbriggan library for their help and encouragement.

A special thanks to the researchers of the RTE programme 'Bookline', whose words indeed inspired me to write the sequel to *Fear of the Collar*, and to the staff and researchers of 'The Late Late Show' for their courtesy and hospitality and for all the letters, which were a great help. Thanks, Gay.

To all the journalists for their many encouraging reviews of my first book, which helped to inspire me. Thank you.

I am beholden most of all to my publishers, Gill & Macmillan, for their kindness, understanding and untiring efforts in making this possible and to their General and Academic Editor, Fergal Tobin, for his help and advice when I required it most, and especially for taking a chance on me.

Prologue

A few days before my eighth birthday I strolled into the Tiller Doyle's tin-roofed shop in Barnacullia to collect the batch loaves for my foster-mother, Brigid Doyle. The Tiller Doyle was a friendly grocer who always had a smile and a welcome for everyone.

As I watched him filling a brown paper bag with sugar from a sack behind the counter, I never suspected that it was to be the last time I'd stand inside the old shop to collect the messages. I looked at old Tessie Downes chatting to Mrs Costello, who lived just beyond the shop, when I overheard Mrs Downes say that the nuns from Eccles Street Convent were next door. On their annual visit, I supposed, to the foster-parents of the wee lads from the orphanage.

I gathered the twenty Honey Bee sweets, which cost one old penny, and thanked Mr Doyle. He smiled at me and said, 'I'll see you tomorrow, Patrick.' I left the shop, not knowing that tomorrow was to be six years away.

As usual I picked at the crusty batch loaf all the way up to the small whitewashed cottage in the hills of Barnacullia, past Sandyford, County Dublin. I placed the bread on the table and instantly noticed a brown paper parcel on a chair by the old black dresser. I looked at Mrs Doyle, who was busy mixing the soda bread, and turned to her daughter, Margaret, who was seated by the open turf fire darning socks for her brothers, John and Edward.

'What's in that parcel, Margaret?' I asked. I thought it was unusual for her not to answer me. As I lay down that night I got no hint that this was to be the last night on which I would close my eyes to sleep in my cosy cottage home.

I had never known my mother, Helen, as she died when I was very young. Nor did I know my father, John Patrick Touher, as he went away to the war in France when I was nine months old; as far as I know he never returned. My mother was too ill to take care of me and left me with the nuns in St Brigid's Convent, Eccles Street, Dublin, opposite the Mater Hospital. Yet I can recall hearing my parents' names being mentioned by my foster-mother.

The little cottage had just two rooms and a pantry. How and where we all slept—the Doyle family, five in all, with me making six—I cannot remember; yet we were comfortable and happy.

THE NEXT MORNING I was woken up by Margaret. She was like a sister to me. As I went to get dressed in my school clothes she said, 'No, no, not them, Patrick, not today.' It was the first sign I got that something was to happen to me. When she pulled open the paper parcel on the bed to reveal its contents I became excited, shouting, 'Are they for me, Margaret? Am I being sent away?' At that moment her mother entered the room and said, 'Enough chat now, son.—Get him prepared well now, Margaret, and come for breakfast.—You're only going to get your tonsils out.' I was shocked.

I had no idea where I was going, all dressed up in new clothes and shoes. I had a strange feeling about the day ahead, and there was an odd silence in the cottage. As Margaret fixed my new tie I pleaded with her, 'Please tell me where I'm going. Is it to hospital?' She nodded. Suddenly she put her arms around me. She was crying. In total silence I finished my breakfast.

Margaret caressed me in a long farewell embrace. 'See him to the car, Maggie. 'Tis nine o'clock. The car will be waiting down the hill.' I turned to face my foster-mother. Her words were few. 'Go now, son. The men are waiting. May God be always with you.' At that moment she unlocked her folded arms. I could feel her strength around me. I couldn't wipe my tears. She whispered, 'Go now, they're waiting.'

As I passed Tessie Downes's cottage I turned to look back once more. I waved at Mrs Downes as Collie, our dog, ran up to me. I was sure I was coming back soon. As I got into the car I shouted happily to Margaret, 'See you soon. Look after Collie for me.' She never answered.

The car pulled up outside the courthouse in Dundrum, and I was quickly met by a tall garda. 'Is this a hospital?' I asked. He smiled, shook his head, and gave me a bar of chocolate. 'It's a courthouse, son. It won't take long.' He was right.

On the stroke of ten I heard a loud voice commanding us to stand for the judge and be silent in the court. I was mesmerised, yet I felt I was enjoying the new experience. Within seconds I heard my name being called. The tall garda put his arm around me as he led me before the judge, who said in his loud, serious voice, 'Patrick Touher, I am sending you to Artane Christian Brothers' Industrial School for a period of six weeks.' How long is six weeks? I wondered.

The car drove slowly up a long avenue, just off the Malahide Road. It was then I got my first look at the bleak grey stone building that faced out, dominating the suburbs of Marino, Donnycarney, and Artane. As I was being led to the main office I asked the driver, 'Is this where I get my tonsils out?' He glanced down at me and said, 'Yes, perhaps you will, son.' And then I'll get back home to Barnacullia, I thought, to Margaret, Edward, and John.

I followed the driver up the stone steps to the office, where a tall elderly man dressed in black, wearing a white collar just like a priest, I thought, gave me a pair of brown scapulars. 'Wear them always, my son,' he said. He gave me a plate of cake, and then he led me down to the parade ground, where I was amazed to see a huge army of boys lined up; and yet I felt a tinge of excitement take hold of me.

Within a moment an older boy came up to me and said, 'I'm a monitor. I'm in charge of new boys. It's part of my duty to show you around. They all call me the Sly.'

'What are they doing marching like that?'

'This is the first division, Pat. There are over eighteen divisions in all, and they go according to age. Those who are over fifteen are in the first division, and those aged seven or eight are in the last division, you see. You'll be put into the eighteenth. 'Tis a big division, with over sixty boys.' I felt confused but excited.

As each division of the enormous boys' army marched by us, stamping their hobnailed boots, I could hear the shout of 'Left, left, left-right-left! Swing them up, there, or you'll face the wall!'

Suddenly I heard music. I looked at the Sly for an explanation. 'That's the jewel in our crown, Pat: our own famous boys' band. You could be in that if you're a good boy.' I stared at him. 'But I'm only here for six weeks, to get my tonsils out, and then I'm going back to my home in Barnacullia!' I was hurt when he roared with laughter and said, 'Oh God, Pat, for goodness' sake stop it. I'll keep that between us, I promise.'

His expression changed. 'Look, Pat, you're here just like I am. No-one gets sent to Artane for a holiday or to get their tonsils out. This is an industrial school, Pat, where if you step out of line or break the rules you'll be severely punished—just like that lad over there lying across the wall, look ...'

I stared in horror as I saw a man flogging a boy across the bare buttocks with a long leather strap. I lost count of the strokes. 'Who's that man?' 'Oh, he's the drill master. They call him Driller the Killer.' For the first time in my life I began to have real fears.

The band marched off the parade ground as the boys kept time to the shouts of 'Left, left, left-right-left! Lift them up higher, higher! Lift those boots or I'll flog the soles of your feet! Left, left, left-right-left!'

We stopped at the end of a long single-storey building. 'That'll be your class, Pat. It's classroom 1. The Brother in charge is called the Hellfire—but have no fears,' he added, 'they're all very hard once you step out of line, so you've only got to do as the Brothers say. Anything else and your backside won't be worth sitting on.'

I felt lost, lonely and desperate as the Sly shouted, 'Come on, Pat, I'll show you to your dormitory and get you dressed out in Artane gear. You look too posh in that fancy suit. You'd be jeered off the parade ground in that!'

I followed the Sly across the huge parade ground, which was like the square in an army barracks. As I stood in the dormitory I was bewildered at the sheer number of neatly made beds. 'There are five dormitories in all,' the Sly told me. 'This one's the smallest. It holds over a hundred beds. The other dormitories are much bigger.' Then he warned me: 'You must remember once you enter the dormitory that all talking is strictly forbidden. You must ask for permission to go to the toilet or to change a comic, and remember that if you wet or soil your sheets to report it to the monitor. If you don't follow my advice you will be forever at the end of a severe flogging.' Only one thing was bothering me. 'How long is six weeks, Sly?' His response left me shattered. 'Eight years, Pat. I'm sorry to be the one to tell you.'

As I tried to sleep I could hear boys crying and the sounds of lads being beaten across their bottoms and shouting for their mothers, while the Brothers on duty marched up and down the passages. That first night in the dormitory I cried rivers and streams for my lost childhood.

IT TOOK ALMOST two years for me to become a hardened

Artaner, and I was glad when my tenth birthday came around in March 1952: not because of birthday presents or a birthday cake and cards—I had never heard of such luxuries in Artane—but because I was to report to the Brother in charge after breakfast, nicknamed the Dood, to be given a job of work. I was to be placed in a new division and a new dormitory and, best of all, to be allowed to take part in parades and the Corpus Christi processions.

I got up that morning as usual at half past six, while the Brother on duty in dormitory 5, nicknamed the Apeman, stood in the centre passage shouting, 'Up, up, you pups! First three rows out to wash. Last two out will face the wall. Bed-wetters report to the monitor at the double. Soilers bring their soiled sheets to the boot room. I'll make you suffer for the poor souls in Purgatory, you filthy wretches! Next three rows out to wash on the double. Last two back will face the wall!'

Though it was my birthday, it was just like any previous morning in Artane. Whether it was your birthday or Christmas Day or there was four feet of snow outside, the regimental system remained the same. Break the rules of silence in dormitory, chapel, toilets or classroom and you were put out to face the wall or, when on parade, sent to the charge room to face the Dood or Driller the Killer.

That morning in 1952 I took my place in my old division, the sixteenth. I had a good feeling about the day ahead. When the Brother in charge shouted, 'By the left, quick march!' I glanced to my right at Quickfart O'Neill and said, 'Thank heavens this is our last day in this division.' 'Yeah, I hear they're lookin' for five or six new boys for the refectory. The Brother in charge is a madman.' 'What's his name?' 'The Drisco.' Suddenly I was frightened, scared of a man I had never met. At Mass I prayed the Dood would send me to the Sewing Room in the Long Hall. But my prayers were not answered. I was sent to work until I was fourteen in the boys' refectory, seven days a week.

I will never forget the noise at meal times in the refectory. As soon as the Brother on duty blew his whistle for us to begin eating we had to shout to be heard. 'Gimme that yang, yeh swine!' 'You nicked my slash, Rasher!' 'Wait'll I get you after, I'll do yeh, yeh bleedin' skunk!' 'I'll give yeh four conkers for a shot o' yang, Jamjar!'

As a hardened Artaner I enjoyed a good punch-up, and meal time was looked upon as 'mill' time, when fights often broke out over trivial things such as the loaf of bread not being divided evenly.

One stormy November night in the refectory when the Hellfire was on duty with the Drisco, Rasher Dunne shouted, 'Looka, will yez, there's a bleedin' big mill over there!' I looked at my pal Oxo Ryan. His smile widened as he said, 'This is it! I've been waitin' for this. I'm gettin' outa this kip.' Within moments, as the punch-up got worse, Oxo was gone. He'll be back in no time, I thought. As Oxo made good his escape the chants grew louder and louder. 'We want out, we want out!' I felt scared, but in true Artane fashion I joined in with the entire eighteen divisions, chanting and banging the table while stamping my hobnailed boots.

When I was ten I felt I was part of the system in earnest. I could take part in parades and go out on Sunday morning walks around Coolock, Santry, Raheny, Whitehall, Donnycarney, Clontarf, and Marino. But I felt strange marching along through these Dublin suburbs with everyone staring at us.

It took all of those first two years for me to grow with the strict military system. In those early days I lay awake for hours at night in dormitory 5 listening to lads crying. They had different reasons for their tears. Some of them who were bed-wetters were flogged in the boot room before going to bed—flogged not just for dirtying the bedclothes but more so for being too slow to report it or not reporting it at all. I was one of those who believed the story that dormitory 5 was haunted by the Devil and that he promised he would return some night to scorch the building. In the early nineteen-

7

sixties in fact it came about. Dormitory 5, along with the cinema, was burned to the ground.

My worst fears were reserved for the classroom. I feared the 'hard men' like the Hellfire, the Lug, the Bucko, the Macker, and the Sheriff, though they could be good also. But in class I was known as a duffer, and I was awful at spelling, writing, and maths. My poor backside was always on fire from the pain of the hard leather.

I HAD BEEN sentenced to eight years in Artane Industrial School for being an orphan. What a crime! But I was not alone in that valley of tears, as so many others cried for their mothers' love, only to be told to shut up by the Hellfire or the Apeman. I found sanctuary in the chapel, and I often stole away from the gang to be alone on cold, wet days in winter. I became emotional at the singing of the Latin Mass, and often wept as the boys' choir sang the beautiful Latin hymns. I escaped too in my dreams. I walked the road from Barnacullia to the old schoolhouse in Sandyford a thousand times as I dreamed of my stolen childhood.

1

Free as a Bird

The morning of 7 March 1958 was special—not simply because it was my sixteenth birthday but because it was the day I was to leave Artane, to stand on my own two feet, to work for my keep and to face reality in a world far removed from what I had been used to for the last eight years.

As I made my bed to perfection I felt a twinge of sadness. I glanced up and there I could see my pal Rasher Dunne, his towel at the ready. He winked at me. I nodded over to Quickfart O'Neill, who smiled and pretended to look busy while we waited for our turn to go into the washroom.

There were long rows of white wash-hand basins. A rack on the wall held the toothbrushes, and I shared mine with a lot of other boys. I dived on a red lump of carbolic soap and scrubbed my hands and face; then I scrubbed my teeth with the same soap and handed my brush to Quickfart. He was delighted. 'Thanks, Collier, you're a pal.' Rasher shouted, 'Can I have it after yeh, Quickfart? I don't aim to be last out. The feckin' Sheriff is on, yeh know.' I paused for a moment to look out the tall windows of the washroom, facing south. I got a glimpse of the outside world—Marino, Donnycarney, and beyond. I realised I'd be out there within a few hours. But instead of feeling good I was frightened. I was not used to change.

'Last two out will face the wall! You'll suffer for the poor souls in Limbo, I promise!' I laughed as I saw Rasher trip over his towel in the rush to get out. Poor Blossom and the Skunk were the last out, and the Sheriff wasted no time in dealing with them. 'Last again, Blossom! You'll have to learn to hurry yourself up. Bend down, tip your toes, boy. Remember the poor souls in Purgatory and Limbo.' He gave him six of the best and a warning. I watched as he told the Skunk to bend over. The lad was a tough sort. He refused to bend over. The Sheriff grabbed hold of him and forced him over the nearest bed a few feet away and flogged the backside off him, to the sound of 'Leave me alone, leave me alone, you swine!'

That morning as the boys' choir sang the Latin hymns I wept openly. I suppose I had simply become a Christian Brothers' boy, and after such a long period in their care I had become institutionalised. I glanced up and I could see the Sheriff singing to his heart's content. I knew he was a dedicated man, like so many of his colleagues.

As we filed out I was stopped by Brother Crowe. He whispered, 'You're leaving us, Collie, after all these years.' Brother Monaghan smiled and held my hand in his. He spoke softly. 'Take good care now, and remember us in your prayers, Collie. Go to Mass and visit the house of God often.' His last few words almost had me in tears. 'I hope we were not too hard on you, Collie.' I stumbled out of the church.

I quickly joined up with my division, which was number 1. The Sly came towards me, smiled, and said, 'Last day, Collier! Soon you'll be free of all this.' Then the Macker blew his whistle for us to march off to the refectory for the first meal of the day.

The Sly shouted, 'By the left, quick march!' The Rasher tipped me; as I glanced at him he said, 'You'll be out soon, Collie. Can I have yer yang?' 'Yeah, certainly, why not?' I said. Suddenly Quickfart said, 'Can I have yer slash, or even yer monyim?' I nodded yes as we marched through the centre doors to the great refectory.

I stared down at the bowl of hot dripping (monyim), the loaf of yang between each four boys, the milky mug of hot slash. I cast my eyes sadly over the long refectory as though it was to say farewell to a part of my life I was certain I would never be allowed to forget.

As the last of the fifteen divisions marched up the centre passage to chants of 'Left, left, left-right-left,' I felt tears in my eyes. I had no thirst or hunger for yang or slash, as my thoughts were elsewhere.

I was brought back to reality when I heard the Sheriff order the Skunk to face the wall. The Drisco approached me and spoke quickly. 'You're leaving us after all these years. How are you going to manage without us?' I wondered that too. As I was about to say 'I don't know,' he reached out his fat hand to say goodbye. I just cried.

The Drisco was a tough, hard brother, short, stocky and with a fierce temper; a difficult man to like or to get to know. As a boy kitchener I liked him and feared him at the same time. When he was in a bad mood he was dangerous, like a mad bull. I quickly thought of times when he punched the head off me or beat me with a long, heavy stick for some silly thing that went wrong in the kitchen, like forgetting to put the sugar in the tea boiler, or salt in the soup; yet I liked him. He was an odd sort of character, I thought. As he gripped my hand I could tell he was being sincere. 'Have you a home to go to now when you get out?' Home, imagine! Home— where's that, I wondered. I said, 'No, sir. I don't know where I'm going, sir.' Suddenly the Sheriff blew his whistle for grace after meals, and the Drisco shouted in his clear Cork accent, 'Good luck now, and may God be with you. I'll say the Rosary for you; and you'll go to Mass and say your prayers now.'

I was shaking all through as I stood for the grace. Rasher said, 'Yeh know, Collie, yeh could stay in me ma's house till yeh get fixed up.' I glanced at him. 'Where's that?' He leaned in to me so as not to be heard. 'Rialto, up in the flats, third floor.' Without warning the second brother on duty, nick-named the Crank, pulled Rasher from behind, punching the head off him and kicking him. He shouted, 'Now face the wall, you filthy tramp. I'll put manners on you, you bad-mannered jackeen.' I felt my heart race, hoping he would not come back for me …

The Sheriff's whistle sounded for march-out. The moni-tors shouted, 'By the left, quick march! Left, left, left-right-left! Lift them up or face the wall!' The Rasher shouted, 'Gimme a chance! I was only prayin', sir, honest I was!' The Crank shouted, 'Bend over the bench. Trousers down. I'll make you pray, boy, on bended knees!' The cries from Rasher as each fierce stroke of the Crank's hard leather crashed across his naked bottom echoed off the refectory walls.

The Sheriff came towards us and we got ready to march as the cries for help from Rasher Dunne faded. I glanced behind me, and for the last time I caught sight of the Sheriff as he clattered a boy across the face so hard that the boy was knocked to the floor. 'He'll burst some lad's eardrums one of these days,' Quickfart shouted. The Skunk responded sharply, 'Yeah, but it won't be bleedin' mine, I swear it. I'm due outa here soon.' 'Yeah, the sooner the bleedin' better,' the Sly retorted as he came towards us, and added, 'If you know what's good for yeh yeh'll keep yer trap shut or yeh'll get what Rasher got, an' I swear to it. Now lift them up. Left, left, left-right-left!'

Some things just never change, I thought as I marched to the parade ground. I had as much fear as ever in me as I swung my arms high and stamped my hobnailed boots as hard as I could, even knowing it was the last time I would have to go through it. I felt as if I was marching in an army, a boys' own army. I was glad when the Sly shouted, 'Halt! At ease! Fall out!'

I was tense and emotional as I stood before the Macker, who was standing with the drill master, Tom Purcell, on parade. They both smiled, shook my hand, and wished me well. As I marched up to the store-room to collect my new suit and working clothes for outside, the thoughts of my first day back in 1950 flooded my mind, when I stood here to get dressed up in Artane clothes and hobnailed boots.

After saying goodbye to my pals and a few Brothers I encountered, I was on my way out of one of the toughest institutions in the country, yet I found it hard to hold back the tears.

I put my hand into my pocket to take out the address Segoogie (Brother Shannon) had given me earlier. He said they would put me up and I would be at home there—but I could have kicked him! The writing was just a scribble. I couldn't make out the home I was to go to, or indeed the address of the bakery I was to work in either. 'Christ, I'm being deserted!' I thought.

It was a long walk from the parade ground to the bus stop on the Malahide Road. I felt utterly alone. A car approached as I passed the old quarry to my right. I noticed two young lads about twelve years old in the back. The driver shouted: 'Could you tell me the way to the main office?' 'Yes, sir, you'll find it on your right, just as you pass the statue of the Sacred Heart.' I glanced at the two boys seated in the back and I couldn't help myself as the tears flowed down my cheeks. I hurried across the Malahide Road and waited anxiously for the bus that would bring me into the future.

I stood at the bus stop opposite the main gates and stared at the great school building that so dominated the area. I looked up at the clear blue sky, and watched a flock of birds flying over. As the number 42 bus pulled up, I smiled and muttered as I hopped on the back, 'Free as a bird!'

I sat downstairs on the bus, clutching my brown paper parcel. Suddenly I heard the conductor shout, 'Fare, son! Where are you going, lad?' My mind was all at sea. The conductor asked again, 'Where are you going, lad?' I spoke quickly. 'Where are you going to?' The conductor looked amazed and spoke sharply. 'The Pillar, mate. It says it on the front, lad. The Pillar in the city centre.' At least I knew where

I was going to get off. I paid my twopence and sat tight.

When I stood up to get off I noticed the conductor staring me up and down. I knew then that I stood out in my Artane clothes. I tried to read the address Segoogie gave me, and I cursed his rotten handwriting. ''Tis worse even than mine!' I glanced about. I noticed a guard gazing at the new spring wear in Clery's window. Filled with apprehension, I spoke quietly to him. 'Please, sir, could you help me find this place? I'm lost, sir.' He looked down at me. He was tall—a double for the Macker, I thought. He smiled at me and led me across the road. We stopped in front of the Palm Grove ice-cream parlour. He didn't ask me if I would like an ice-cream cone: he simply went in and got me one. I was lost for words, but to me his kindness was the mark of a great man.

He hadn't asked me where I came from, and I began to wonder why, but I shouldn't have bothered. As I followed him to the corner where the *Irish Press* office stood in Middle Abbey Street, he stopped and said, 'You're from Artane School, son?' He smiled, and I nodded to him in response. Then he pointed to the place where I was to stay. 'You're home, son. I'm sure they'll take care of you.' Then he nodded and disappeared into the crowd. For a long moment I stood staring emptily after him.

I looked up at the tall red-brick building. The sign over it read *The Catholic Boys' Home*. It did not impress me. I was frightened. I felt out of my depth. I just wanted to go home to Artane.

I found it difficult to hold back the tears as I walked up the few steps. There was a long room in front of me, and I could smell the tea being prepared. There were two long dining tables with white cloths—a miniature Artane refectory, I thought. I heard voices. A door opened on my right. 'Come this way, boy.' I stood in the office, nervously gazing at the cream-painted walls. An elderly man came to meet me. 'So you're the new boy from Artane.' I half smiled and said, 'Yes, sir. I got lost.' He looked me in the eye and spoke with a warmth I had rarely known. 'Many have done the very same thing, my boy. A darn pity a Brother doesn't come with you. Perhaps they're too busy, son.' After a few weeks I was to realise just why they didn't come with us.

The Catholic Boys' Home was mainly for boys aged sixteen and over. It was a kind of stopping-off place in the city for boys who had left school and had no home to go to. We paid seven shillings and sixpence a week for our keep. The food was very basic and no better than what we were used to in Artane. But we did have hot showers.

I remember that first evening at tea quite clearly. I sat down with lads whom I spent years with in Artane—some of whom I didn't like. The first nickname I heard being shouted was 'Brown Tango'—an African chap in his late teens or a bit older. He lorded it a bit, and perhaps he thought he was better than us from Artane. I didn't like the look he gave me, and I believe he bumped against me on purpose, to knock my mug of tea out of my hand. He certainly threw himself about. Oddly enough, the ex-Artaners were not like that.

It was typical Artane food: bread and margarine and a mug of sweet tea in the evening; breakfast had one change, which was a bowl of porridge. I was shown to my dormitory on the third floor. The front of the dormo looked out onto Middle Abbey Street; the back looked down into the North Lotts, where we watched couples courting and fondling each other at night among the winos. From my bedside I could see the clock over the *Irish Independent* office, and I was happy about that, because I had never had a watch!

I'll never be able for this noise, I told myself through my tears. I cried as much now as ever I did for my lost childhood, tears of loneliness and self-pity. There was no real sense of being free. The dormitory had two long rows of beds made of tubular steel and painted grey. The walls were painted yellow and dark green. As I put away my few belongings I was dreading the future. I just wanted to go out and get the bus back to Artane.

The lads acted in a boisterous way, and at times many

were very rowdy. I was shocked later to see lads from Artane running up and down naked, some of them fondling or messing about with their private parts and generally showing off to others how big their penis was! This was a totally new experience for me.

I got off the bed as a lad came towards me. It was Fatser Boylan. 'Want me to show yeh the city? Come on.' I looked at him. I remembered the day he broke my nose over a silly matter in 1955. I had gone to the Brother in charge on parade, who was the Sheriff. He had snapped at me sharply. 'What do you want me to do, Cauliflower?' His next remark stayed with me for ever. 'Stand up for yourself, boy. Be brave and hit back or kick back twice as hard.'

As the days passed I began to find my way around the city. We were brought to services in the Pro-Cathedral: sodality, the Rosary, and Benediction. Hearing again the choir singing the Latin hymns moved me emotionally, making me more homesick for Artane. As I stood up after the Benediction was over, the man in charge of us in the boys' home said, 'Confessions are being heard now.' I better go, I thought.

When I entered the confessional my mind raced over the past few weeks. Gosh, I've nothing to confess, I said to myself. It's a waste of time.

I heard the little hatch go across. I smiled, as I had no bad thoughts and had committed no dirty deeds. The middle-aged priest spoke clearly. 'How long since your last confession?' 'Not long, father: a few weeks.' The priest continued, 'Well, lad, what have you got for me? Anything to confess?'

'No, father.' And I thought that was that.

As though he didn't believe me, he raised his deep voice. 'Do you attend all services: Mass, Holy Communion, novenas, and your sodality?'

'Yes, father, at all times, father.' I thought that was it, but soon I was to be confused. The priest grunted. 'Ah, sure, 'tis too good, lad, you are. Tell me, do you use swear-words?'

'No, father, the Brothers taught us not to, sir.'

'Do you play with yourself at all?'

16

'No, father. I play with others, though.'

'Tell me, do you see the others play with themselves at all?'

I was baffled. 'You mean in the snooker room or in the park?' He raised his voice, angrily I thought. 'No, damn it, anywhere, boy! Did you see them play with their bodies?'

Suddenly the thought struck me. 'Yes, father, quite often.'

'Where did all this take place, my son?'

'Oh, mostly up in the dormitory, and at times in the shower room, father. I could never understand it, though.'

'I see, I see ... I'll have to visit there. 'Tis better that you don't understand, lad, as it will only corrupt your mind. And remember to continue to go to Holy Mass and all the services. 'Tis a *mortal sin* to perform dirty acts with another, to indulge in self-abuse of your own body for enjoyment or fulfilment. Remember to keep your hands joined when temptation strikes. It's Satan's way of corrupting the mind. Now for your sins, say five decades of the Rosary and do the Stations of the Cross at least once a week.'

I FOUND GOING back to visit Artane a great relief, and each time I came away I could see the gulf between being inside and living outside. In the late summer of 1958 I visited Button Your Shirt—Brother Charles. He didn't look a day older. He was a gentleman first and foremost. He walked me down to the tailors' workshop, and offered to have a new top coat made for me. I agreed. There and then the boys got to work and measured me for it. I knew a few of the lads. Skin the Goat and Skinnymalink were put in charge of the proceedings. I wore that overcoat with pride as soon as winter came. It cost me three pounds ten shillings—a lot of money to me, as I was earning two pounds a week and had to pay for my digs out of it.

It was August that year, when I was walking out of a shop on the Malahide Road, that I met the Brother who was called the Bogman. I got a lump in my gut as he approached me. He was one of the hardest and cruellest Christian Brothers I ever came in contact with. He spoke loudly. 'Collie, how are you keeping?' 'Fine,' I replied, but I was thinking of the cold winter's day on the long icy slides as he stood urging us to go down on our hunkers in case we fell, when suddenly he drew out and clattered Rasher Dunne across the face. Poor Rasher was knocked flying down the slide on his back. I recall asking the Bogman, 'Why did you do that? He's done nothing.' The Brother had simply withdrawn, looked sorry, and apologised. That's the way it was with them.

As I SETTLED down in my new home I found it difficult to shake off the shackles of Artane. I frequently walked in my sleep and had dreadful nightmares. I dreamt of the time the Hellfire locked an eight-year-old boy in the press, with his trousers hanging from the blackboard, because he wet himself. It took years of travel for me to get over those nightmares.

I was glad about some aspects of the boys' home. I had my own toothbrush, soap, and towel—a big change from sharing with forty others. I kept going to church services; I was an emotional and institutionalised ex-Artaner, out of my depth in a big city—though I was finding my feet.

I got to know and love Hector Grey. I stood with him on many a Sunday morning as he sold alarm clocks, watches, and all sorts of things. Many of the clocks worked for years; some lasted until the following Sunday, when customers brought them back. Outside the Dublin Woollen Mills on the corner of Lower Liffey Street and Lower Ormond Quay was his favourite spot, often called at the time 'Hector's Corner'.

I began to fall in love with the city. I walked along Bachelor's Walk on summer evenings, dreaming of what I wanted to be. I knew I was not cut out for bakery work or rising before dawn for the rest of my life. I was driven by a desire to be someone great—to achieve greatness. I prayed as I was taught to pray for all my needs.

I wanted to be a singer, but even the Apeman told me I

couldn't sing for farthings. I remember the day I was made to stand on top of the table in classroom 4. The Sheriff was looking for boys to join the choir. I was told to sing 'The Rising of the Moon', while the remainder of the class were told to stand up and stamp their feet. I was pulled off the table and told by the Sheriff to shut up and in future during singing to study poetry!

I began to take a closer look at myself, especially when I was out in the city alone. I took note of how other teenagers dressed, and it wasn't long before I realised that I could never really look much different in my Artane Sunday outfit, a heavy serge suit. I longed to have the money but I wondered how I could get enough of it.

One thing that I was certain about and that was that I was in some way different from the other ex-Artaners with whom I shared the same poor facilities in the Catholic Boys' Home. I was a bit of a loner, and rather choosy about who I mixed with. I was old-fashioned in my ways and I was very particular about my cleanliness and how I appeared to others.

I carried the shadow of Artane like a crown of thorns.

I longed for a united, free Ireland; I prayed at night for my wonderful vision of a nation once again. This patriotic spirit was fostered in me from my earliest time in Artane. I fancied myself as a leader who would bring this about, and in my dreams I was Patrick Pearse.

2
Buttermilk and Apple Pie

On my first day at work I got the early bus out to Fairview, carrying with me the handwritten note Brother Shannon had given me. I showed it to the conductor, and he let me off at Edge's Corner.

I felt I was out in the country. I looked about and saw the sign over a shop: *Milk—Dairy—Brennan's*. I went in, and there began a friendship that lasted until Bill Brennan sold the shop in the late seventies. I began to feel a certain amount of relief when suddenly a big stout woman entered the shop. She spoke rather loudly and abruptly, I thought. 'Are you from Artane Industrial School, boy?' As I looked down at my shoes and clothes I supposed they told it all. She reached out her fat hand. Her grip was firm and she left butter on my fingers. 'I'm Mrs Brennan. They're expecting you in the bakery. You'll like Mr Bradley. He's a countryman from Derry.' She looked at me. 'I suppose you're from Dublin?' 'No, ma'am, I'm from Artane School.' She smiled and said, 'Bill will take you to the bakery, son.' She reminded me of Brigid Doyle in Barnacullia.

For a few moments I stood gazing at the place in which I was to begin my working life. What a bleak-looking house, I thought as I entered the yard. On my left was a well-kept lawn, and the garden had a spring freshness about it, with tall palm trees on my left, then the bakery. I became apprehensive now as I heard male voices shouting very crude and vulgar words, and some I had never heard before. My mind was filled with all sorts of fears.

I heard a man's voice with a northern accent. 'Hello, son. Are you the new boy from Artane?' On top of the old stone steps that led into the house stood a very tall middle-aged man, who was to be my first employer. He was quite friendly; I began to feel tears welling in my eyes. 'Come on in, son, and tell us about yourself and Brother Shannon.'

Mr Bradley seemed huge as I stood looking up at him in the front room: taller than the Sheriff and even the Macker, I reckoned. 'Are you ready, Pauline? I want you to meet our new baker from Artane.' I shook hands with his wife, who looked young and very attractive. I was taken by surprise when she held me and gave me a hug and a friendly kiss on the cheek. Her smile and warmth made me long for a mother's love. 'Now you'll have some breakfast with us before my husband brings you down to meet the lads. They're both ex-Artane lads, and they're both from Dublin, like myself.' I sat down to the first bacon, sausage and egg breakfast I had ever seen.

I was a little apprehensive about working with ex-Artaners. I had so many fears about my future that I had never realised existed when I was in Artane. We were not properly prepared for the outside world—except for work: from the age of ten I had worked seven days a week. Though discipline and hard work stood me well in later years, I found out the hard way that a baker's life was not an easy one.

Eddie Kavanagh was a fair-haired young man in his twenties, a Dublin lad from Whitehall. I got on with Eddie much more than with Matt, his deputy, who came from the inner city. I was treated like an errand boy by the bakers. When Matt ran out of cigarettes he would order me to go out and look for as many butts as I could find around Fairview, and often I would stop a person and beg a cigarette from them. Knowing Matt, I was afraid to come back without any.

The work itself wasn't hard, though I found it monotonous, and the baking powder gave me a runny nose and head colds. The hours were short, but getting up so early made each day seem long. Sometimes the bakers would start work at three in the morning, and I'd have to be in at half four. Getting up so early made me cranky.

But within a few months I was settling down to the way of things. I can clearly recall those early days, stirring the buttermilk left in big tall milk churns by Merville Dairies. After the bake I often sat on a bag of soft Boland's flour and ate a chunk of white griddle bread and home-made apple pie.

Home now was a shared dormitory with over twenty ex-Artane boys. Life in the boys' home was nothing to boast about. There were far too many fights for my liking, and theft was rife. There was no place to put away our personal belongings, and we simply had to sleep on whatever little money we had earned.

I was abused and assaulted by the tough guy from Tanganyika known as Brown Tango. I was having a shower one Saturday morning when out of the blue he got in beside me and rubbed up against me. I pushed him away. Suddenly he went for me and punched me so hard all over my body that I had to fight—Artaner style! I pulled his hair, kicked and pulled at him to knock him over, but I ended up pleading for help as he fought like a tiger. He was just too strong. Help came from a few lads I knew who were passing. I lived in fear of Brown Tango, more than I ever feared even Driller the Killer. I was assaulted many times after that, and I was forever having to defend myself, as though I attracted trouble.

Once a few lads I knew well from Artane were messing in the dormitory with a lad's private parts. When I walked in one of them was sitting on his back, by way of holding him down on the floor. I could see his bare bottom. I asked without thinking, 'What are you doing to him, Macker?' He looked at me. He was sure of himself. He had worked as a cook for the Brothers in Artane. Suddenly, without warning, I was surrounded. 'Right, lads, we've got him. Take them off!' I was pushed over the bed, half naked. There was silence for a moment, as someone was mauling my naked bottom. I believed they were all only messing when this guy who was not an ex-Artaner shouted, 'He's got a smashin' bottom. I'll have it.' I didn't know what was happening, but a lad from Sandyford, Mick Cranny, suddenly entered the room and shouted, 'Stop! Don't! Stop it! Don't do that to him—he's my friend.' They let me up. I was shocked to see this guy with a penknife. 'What were you goin' to do with that?' 'You're real lucky, Collier: I was about to have a piece o' your bum.'

ALL WAS NOT well at work either, as I couldn't relate at all to people who were not ex-Artaners, while I had no idea about girls. I often irritated the men. Eddie complained that I talked too much and sang too many of the songs I learnt in school: I had formed a habit of whistling or singing 'The Croppy Boy' and 'The Boys of Wexford'. One day I couldn't stop laughing at Mick Bradley as he was making griddle bread with Eddie, and he spoke seriously to me about my ways. 'One day, Pat, you're going to find a great deal of trouble, the way you go on here, singing and laughing when spoken to. You give the impression that you either have a wee chip on your shoulder or that you're odd.'

As I went home that evening I felt ashamed at what Mr Bradley had said. I wasn't whistling as I walked either. I began to realise that I was not wanted.

The thoughts of being rejected frightened me. Normally an ex-Artane lad who was rejected because he did not fit in was returned to Artane if he had no family to look after him. Being an orphan, I would have had to return, as I would not be able to pay for my keep. That night as I lay down to sleep I felt unwanted, but I prayed as I had learnt to pray in Artane. I made up my mind that I would not be going back. I knew I could fight to achieve that end, and, thank God, I did. I was bitterly determined to succeed.

BY THE END of 1958 I was more settled in work. I felt I was

part of something, though it was a case of the men in the bakery simply getting used to me. Mrs Bradley was very kind. She must have felt sorry for me. She brought me into the house some evenings to feed me. How I loved that!

I walked to work from the boys' home to the little bakery in Fairview, getting up at about four, with no breakfast, just a few 'prairie sandwiches' to take with me. The lads often had no lunch with them, and Eddie and Matt would be glad to share mine. Eddie would often remark, 'For Jesus' sake, Pat, could they not find a bloomin' thing to put in them?'

I liked Eddie, though often he'd get ratty with me. A favourite expression of his was 'Look, Paddy, for feck's sake, d'yeh want me to lose me rag? Do yeh?' Matt was quite something else. He showed all the signs of an Artaner. He enjoyed ordering people about, and he loved his authority; he spoke down to everyone when there were people about. He was more at home and normal when he found himself in trouble, as when Eddie would not come in to work. Matt would need me to pull him through, and he was a better bloke then.

One day I was working with the boss and Eddie. During tea break neither Mick nor Eddie had anything to eat with them. We never stopped for long, as there was always bread or whatever it was to come out of the oven. I was the only one who brought lunch with me. The boss looked at me. I was apprehensive about offering him some of my prairie sandwiches. Mick glanced at me. Putting down the cup he said, 'God damn it, Pat, can I have one?' Eddie laughed. I watched as Mick opened the bread up. 'Is this all they feed you with? Damn shame.' He looked me in the eye and spoke softly. 'You know, son, you'll have to find a real home. You're living far too long with Artane.' 'He reeks of Artane!' Eddie shouted. 'You need a good woman to sort you out Pat,' Mick said, as he turned to face Eddie. 'What do you think?' Eddie almost choked on his Woodbine, and then responded, 'If there was a room in my place me ma would look after him. Mick reacted instantly. 'Ah, sure, 'tis the old story, Eddie. If I had the money I'd buy you a jar. If only I had this and that, I'd do wonders, Eddie.'

Some days later I was asked to do the garden and paint the bakery windows, as there was not enough work in the bakery for the three of us. I was asked to come up for tea by Pauline. I began to get the feeling for real home life as I made myself comfortable. Mick Bradley asked me if I'd like to see around. How could I say no? It all came back to me as I stood in their large bedroom. Imagine, I thought, what it would be like to sleep in a nicely painted room all to myself, with carpet on the floor. I knew then that I'd have to change. As I meandered home from the Bradleys' house I felt happy within myself but realised that that kind of happiness is too instant, and once I got into the boys' home I was back to earth.

It was the wishes of the Board of Management that we should look for proper lodgings, and we were encouraged not to make the hostel our permanent home. There was no television to enjoy after work. I played hurling and football for O'Toole's GAA club, though I began to like soccer, the forbidden sport in my schooldays. I loved playing the matches that were quickly organised by our soccer fanatics Mick Cranny and Des O'Reilly.

As I recall, there was no such thing as unemployment pay or dole. All Artaners were skilled tradesmen and, what's more, we didn't mind hard work or getting up early. This stood us well in tough times.

The Catholic Boys' Home became a meeting place for Artaners who lived in digs or who had joined the army. I knew of many lads at the time who lost their jobs and found it hard to deal with people or to fit in, who simply got fed up and joined the army. Many went to England to join up. But wherever they chose to go they brought their skills with them, without which I believe many would have fallen by the wayside.

I met an old pal, Boohie Kelly, and I wondered why he was so pleased with himself. 'Where are you working?' I asked him. 'Oh, I'm in the School of Music and I'm going into the army.' I should have felt happy for him but my heart ruled my head and I felt sorry for myself. As I walked up O'Connell Street my mind went back to the time he got me into the Artane Boys' Band. Why couldn't I be like Boohie? I cursed Brother Joe O'Connor under my breath for pulling me out of the band.

As well as going to the cinema regularly I went to the gods in the Theatre Royal every Sunday night with a gang of lads. It cost one and ninepence—less than ten pence in today's money. For that we got a stage show that has never been bettered. We also had our own show going on up in the gods: shouts of 'Where's Rasher? What'yeh doin'?' 'I'm watchin' your man's mot—what'yeh bleedin' think I'm doin'!'

A seat up in the gods was quite far away from the stage, so trying to even see what the star looked like was expecting too much for your one and nine, never mind trying to hear the jokes. To me the jokes and the skit up in the gods were all part of the enjoyment.

In September 1958 Dublin got to the All-Ireland final in Croke Park. My boss, Mick Bradley, was on a high. The bakery was decked out in the red-and-white colours of Derry and the blue of Dublin. I didn't see Mick for a few weeks after Dublin's great victory. When I did see him he was on crutches. I heard he broke his leg trying to climb a wall outside Croke Park to get in to the game.

In those days I was an ardent Dublin supporter. I recall seeing the Macker, the Sheriff and a few more Brothers at the games. On many an occasion ex-Artaners, especially those living in Sheriff Street and the Catholic Boys' Home, threw apples or bottles at the Brothers. The Sheriff got hit on many occasions, yet it never changed him one bit. It hurt me to see the Brothers being attacked like that. It was never my attitude.

IT WAS ON the August holiday Monday in 1958 that I paid a nostalgic visit to the Doyles up in Barnacullia. I set off early from the home with my old pal Des O'Reilly, having borrowed Fatser Boylan's bike, as Dessie had decided he would like to make a day of it and leave after breakfast.

I loved Dublin city centre, especially on Sunday mornings before the hustle and bustle began. I loved the feeling I gained from being able to choose what I wanted to do. For me, Dublin before ten on a holiday or a Sunday morning was heaven to meander through.

We decided to stop at the old schoolhouse in Sandyford and take a walk around the playground before turning up the old road to Barnacullia and Glencullen. We put away our bicycles at O'Neill's pub—now the Blue Light. Locks and chains were not necessary then. We walked the road, up to the old grocer himself, the Tiller Doyle. Bald on top, a touch of silver along the sides, he shouted out: 'I remember ye, boys. Oh, God be good to those who return to thank those who cared for them!' He turned to Dessie. 'You're the O'Reilly lad. I well remember you, boy, and Mrs Downes. Oh, God be good to her.' I could see he was becoming affected now as his eyes became moist. 'I suppose you'll go up to Carty's Green to see Roseanna.' Dessie nodded yes.

I slipped quietly away. I said goodbye in a whisper, but never did the words mean so much. All my childhood dreams and fond memories came flooding to my mind as I left. I could only nod to Dessie as we walked up the climb until we reached the turning of the road that led up to the row of cottages on the hill. The track, as we called it when we lived there, was still the same. I stopped at the well where as a young boy I fetched buckets of water for Brigid and Roseanna Fay Doyle and for their great neighbour Mrs Downes. I could see that Dessie was gazing down the hill and across to Carty's Green. I knew that he was reliving his lost childhood, as I was.

Mrs Doyle looked as healthy as ever as I put my arms around her. I wondered where Margaret and her brother John were. Before I could ask, in walked Margaret, followed by John—tall, thin but strong-looking, and smiling. As I greeted them, Margaret first, my heart missed a beat. As I turned to shake John's hand I couldn't believe how much older than me he looked. I just smiled and cried with joy. I thought of so much that day, of Margaret as my loving sister, and how I wished to God that she was.

3

Home Again

I was having a fair number of problems in the Catholic Boys' Home towards the end of my first year there. I knew I had to start looking for digs, but I had another problem, one that was to cause me a great deal of bother throughout my life, and that was money, or the lack of it.

I was looking for digs with Fatser Boylan. We were up near the Phoenix Park, at a big red-bricked house. I got frightened and told Fatser to go up to the house without me. He shouted, 'Paddy, we're up—come on, will yeh!' The big hall door opened, and a tall woman with a Cork accent said, 'It's £2 7s 6d per week sharing for full board. Laundry will be two shillings a week extra.' Well, I roared laughing and ran. I was earning only £2 5s 6d a week for working six days, even though it was rarely more than six hours a day. I knew I could never afford to move into fancy lodgings.

Carmella O'Grady, who acted as my adopted godmother while I was in Artane, was an educated and elegant woman, as were her daughters, Joan, Carine, and Elizabeth—far and away too educated for Minnie (Billy Kelly) and my other pals. Carmella's only son, Alan, followed his father's footsteps in becoming a doctor. I had visited the O'Gradys every Saturday since I left Artane and I was allowed to bring pals from the home.

It was January 1959. Christmas had not been great, but a

29

visit to the O'Gradys in Ballsbridge was a highlight, and, like all visits before, it was a lovely occasion. Whenever Minnie came out with me he generally broke down laughing, so much so that Carmella was amazed one Saturday as she served tea on the lawn to see Minnie with tea pouring down his nostrils! I was just as bad. I remember Dr O'Grady standing there looking at the pair of us. He was a fine, well-built and elegant man. Carine was concerned now as she spoke to us. 'What's so funny, Patrick? Is it us, or something we said?' How could I tell her that it was!

I explained that Minnie and I tended to laugh at a lot of things that were strange to us, and indeed the whole concept of having tea on the lawn to us ex-Artaners was simply too much to take. As I look back on the style of things at the O'Grady home in Anglesea Road, it does tend to bring a smile. In some ways they did help me to be ambitious and to style myself like them. I knew I could never be like them, but at least I found that the more time I spent in their company, the more I would learn from their ways.

It the early spring of 1959 I was lonely and sick with toothache and gum disease, which I had suffered a lot with in Artane. I was sleepwalking often too, as were many other lads. I regularly woke up in some other chap's bed. On one occasion I woke up lying naked on top of this chap who slept at the far end of the dormitory. He was known as Danno, a fine, dark-haired handsome chap, not an ex-Artaner. He had his arms wrapped around me and he was talking in his sleep. Well, I was scared, yet I felt good. I had never had any sexual experience or desires nor ever had an orgasm, and I was almost seventeen. I had seen on many occasions lads in the showers doing things to each other, which I had no experience of but which I liked watching them do.

I once had a shower with Danno. He spoke with a soft, educated Dublin accent. 'Hold mine and I'll hold yours.' I have to admit that I did as he requested, for good reasons too. The last time I had refused to come to a lad's aid was my first meeting with the Brown Tango, and I was badly beaten up by him. What astonished me about this new guy who had suddenly appeared was that he was a member of the Jehovah's Witnesses organisation. He never came near me again, though. I could not have pleased him, as I was still very naïve in those matters.

Because of my toothache I stayed out of work for the first time in the twelve months I was in the bakery. I went back to bed after my visit to the dentist, having had two or more teeth extracted, and I lay there listening to the sound of the traffic below my window in Middle Abbey Street. I could tell whether it was a car, bus or lorry that was passing. My face was out of shape and I felt alone and dumped, like a little boy in the woods.

I was gazing at the high ceiling when I heard heavy footsteps. God, I thought, it couldn't be the Sheriff or the Apeman calling! But it was my boss, Mick Bradley. I felt awful. Tears were never too far away; and as I write this I can still see the big man from Derry, so tall and straight, red-faced, looking down at me; and his look said it all. 'I was concerned, Pat. You never miss work. Damn it, Pat, someone could have let us know. Pauline was very concerned, so I dropped in. The lads will be in later.' He paced the floor, as though not knowing what to do.

He pulled up an old green steel chair. He spoke quickly now, as though he wanted to go. 'Look, Pat, this is no fit place for a lad like you. I'll see to it you get a nice homely person to put you up, preferably in Fairview.' Suddenly a few big lads entered the dormo, shouting. I recognised at once the loudest voice. It was Brown Tango. 'You sick or somethin', Collier?' He stood a few feet from my boss. I just nodded. I hated the sight of him. Brown Tango got smart and shouted, 'Who's the big redneck, Collier?' I responded, 'He's my boss.' 'I hope he's fuckin' payin' for you bein' out sick!' He came closer now, and the gang came with him. 'We'll have a nice warm shower together, Collie—perhaps when you're better. I need it badly.' Just at that my boss stood up in front of Tango, who looked surprised at how tall he was.

He backed off. Suddenly the caretaker appeared, shouting at the lads to get out and find a day's work and not be seen in the dormitory during the day.

Mick looked down at me. 'I'll have you out of here within a week, Pat. I'm glad I saw you like this.' As he left, I cried and smiled. I was happy.

A few days later I was on the move, thanks to Mick Bradley and his wife. Later in the bakery Mick gave me an address: 17 Cadogan Road, Fairview. After being told how close it was to the bakery, I couldn't wait to get there. As I went to leave that day, Pauline called me into the house. She began to advise me on how to behave—that it would be a new start for me. She never asked me if I would like tea or something to eat: she was the sort of person who would simply prepare the food and put it in front of you. She had a lovely way about her—homely and caring, and a real down-to-earth Dublin woman.

As I got up to leave, her words were most encouraging. 'You'll like the Mooneys. They're Dublin folk. Let me know how you get on, and if you have any problems come to me, Pat.' I was away on a hack to find my new home.

Number 17 Cadogan Road was only a few hundred yards from the Bradleys in Windsor Avenue, Fairview. As I entered the road I stood gazing down along the rows of red-brick terraced houses, with their six-foot front gardens all railinged off with neatly coloured painted gates, and all with matching laced curtains. Number 17 had a cream-coloured door, with small panes of beautifully coloured leaded glass. The door opened and I was greeted by Mrs May Mooney. She hugged me and led me into the sitting-room, saying, 'You're most welcome. You're home now, son.'

Mrs Mooney spoke with a nice soft Dublin accent and quickly made me feel at home, and I was treated like one of the family. She had one child, Lorcan, who was doing his finals in St Joseph's, Fairview. I shared a room with Lorcan, and he got so annoyed with my early rising that he once threw my alarm clock out the window. He hated the sound of loud ticking clocks in his bedroom—and so did I. I had to find all sorts of hiding-places for the clock. Sometimes when it went off at half four I would have forgotten where I had hidden it.

Once I put the clock outside on the window ledge, just above the kitchenette, which had a glass roof. When I pulled up the window I tried to grab the Hector Grey clock with its bell on top. I knocked it and it crashed through the glass below. I promised I'd build Mrs Mooney a shed for the trouble I caused. I did, and it blew down in the first big wind. 'God help the girl that gets you, Pat,' she said.

I soon realised how different home life was from sleeping with over forty boys in a dormitory in the hostel or with two hundred boys in the dormitories in Artane, which was still to leave its deep shadow on me. But I also realised that I was out of my depth in the small terraced house. I found it difficult to relate to the family. The things I would talk about, I found they had no interest whatsoever in. At times I'd be told to shut up, though not in an aggressive way. Lorcan often tried to help me change my ways but it had no real effect. I knew he meant well, and he was studying hard. He found less time to pay any attention to me. I suppose I annoyed people quite a bit in those days, yet Lorcan never really got angry with me. He regularly treated me to a one-and-one—fish and chips—for supper.

His father, Bill Mooney, was a tall, slim man. He liked his pint, and enjoyed it better when he shared one with my boss and the lads. Bill was to be seen quite a bit around the bakery, especially on a Sunday morning. I went to work on Sundays with Matt and Eddie, just for a few hours. I remember going up Windsor Avenue to the local shops and down Philipsburgh Avenue to the Pear Tree and along to Fairview Strand, delivering the pure hot buttermilk soda bread. I was given a real Dublin fry-up by Mrs Bradley; it made Sunday work all the more special.

I began going out at night with lads I'd met in the boys' home. I soon realised that their company did not suit me at all. I was away from that system at last, and slowly I was beginning to change. I went to my first dance in the Irish Club in Parnell Square. It was a céilí and old-time. I was awful with girls. I simply wanted to learn how to dance, and honestly I did not realise I could ask them out. I just believed they had to dance with me once I got up and asked them. Within a few weeks I was quite good at the old-time waltz, and I had the same partner I had begun with in the old-time waltz competition for the Mícheál O'Hehir Cup. It never dawned on me to ask my dance partner out. I had no idea about dating girls, or about sex for that matter.

I began to enjoy life. The simple things pleased me most, like a walk in the park, which was only a hundred yards from the house. I enjoyed a game of football, hurling, or soccer. To these were added my new pastime of going to dances. The Irish Club became my favourite haunt; but I still went to the Theatre Royal on Sundays for my seat up in the gods. It was my joy, and I loved treating myself. On Sunday nights it was simply terrific to have your ticket and be one of the three thousand in the audience.

It was the custom to book a ticket for the cinemas on Sunday night, and every cinema within two miles of the city centre would be booked out for Sunday nights. I was never one to be caught out without a ticket, as I could never have afforded to buy one on the black market. Cinema tickets were snapped up quickly by the black marketeers by mid-week. But nothing has ever surpassed the Theatre Royal for pure entertainment; and no sooner was one show over than all I'd be talking and thinking about was booking for the next. When I look back to those days, in the late 1950s, I smile at the things that made me happy.

I WAS STILL sleepwalking and having nightmares. I woke up in the wardrobe on several occasions, and other times I found my sheets and pillow on the gas cooker, while I was fast asleep downstairs in the bath. I often woke up fully dressed in bed, although I had taken off my clothes before getting in. In my dreams I was one of the Bold Fenian Men, marching with the Boys of Wexford behind the Artane Boys' Band. I was wakened at three by Lorcan Mooney one morning with a crack of his shoe for shouting, 'Left, left, left-right-left! Lift them up, you pups, or you'll all face the wall!'

I was working very short hours in the little bakery. Approaching the end of my first year out of Artane, I believed I was on the road to nowhere in particular. The bakery business was not a great job to be in—working all hours or none at all. Bill Mooney decided to make a personal attempt to get me into the Bakers' Union. He had tried to explain to me why they could not accept Artane boys. 'You see, Pat, the bakers who work in Boland's, Johnston Mooney's, Kennedy's and O'Rourke's have all served their four years' apprenticeship. They then went to the tech in Kevin Street a number of days or nights each week until they were finished and got their papers.' It was a father-to-son closed shop, just like Bill Mooney's job. He was a printing worker, and, as he told me, no-one could gatecrash into the Printers' Union.

Bill read a letter he had received from Mr Flanagan, the secretary of the Bakers' Union, expressing his sympathy with me and how he felt so sad for ex-Artaners, who were indeed well trained but, as I thought, undesirables.

My boss's business was in trouble, and I had been told I might have to go. Matt had already left. I went to see Mr Flanagan in the union on a number of occasions after that to plead my case, but to no avail. Then one day in early 1959 as I stood before Mr Flanagan, he looked me in the eye and declared that perhaps he could do something for me. It was a great relief to hear him say so.

'Well, Pat, I've got news for you.' I was delighted and relieved that I would not have to go to England. 'We are prepared to allow in a number of non-union lads like yourself who for various reasons did not serve their time under the auspices of the Bakers' Union'—in other words ex-Artaners. I was thrilled, but only for a few moments, as he continued: 'There are two conditions. One is that you pay a fee to join the union.' Good, I thought. I couldn't wait to hear the other. 'The second one is that your father must be in the union and be a fully paid-up member.' I just laughed!

When I told him, Bill shrugged his square shoulders, smiled, and put his arm around me as though I were his son. 'Come on, son. Let's take a walk. I'll treat you to a one-and-one when we get to the chipper in Fairview.' I walked home with Bill up the North Strand. Suddenly he said, 'I hope you don't mind me calling you son. If only May and I could have got you years ago we would have put you through St Joseph's School in Fairview.' I felt like crying, and wished to God he was my dad.

It was around this time or shortly afterwards that Bill began to explain the facts of life to me. We were together in the house and he had brought in a one-and-one. 'If I'd known you'd be home, son, I'd have brought you one. As the tea is brewed now you can have some o' mine. Anyway, the bleedin' queue at the chipper is desperate.' 'I know, Bill. Cafolla's is always packed. Their one-and-ones, though, are smashin'.'

I noticed Bill looking at me, and I could tell there was something on his mind. Suddenly he said, 'Look, son, did the Brothers tell you anything about life: I mean the facts about babies, men and women—that sort of thing?' I began to laugh, and I became flushed. 'No, Bill, but I'd like to know.' I watched anxiously as he lit up a Player's Drumhead cigarette. 'A pity May's not here. Look, son, it takes two to do it, know what I mean, like?' I nodded to him, although I didn't really understand. 'You see, son, some women have lots o' kids. You might wonder why we have only one and some women can't have any at all, you know.' He was almost eating the cigarette at this stage. The small sitting-room was clouded in smoke. I was in bits. Suddenly he said, 'There are things you should know about girls, Pat.' I was scared. I got ready to run as poor Bill looked awful, as though he was in shock. He was having a terrible time trying to come out with it. Then he splurted out the words 'Intercourse, son,' when the door suddenly opened. He said hurriedly, 'Some other time, or perhaps the priest will explain to yeh in more detail than I could.' I laughed at poor Bill. It was part of my nature to behave in that way.

I didn't realise then that Bill was having his own problems with his job and his own personal problems. He never got around to finishing the conversation on life with me. It was some time after that that he told me he had to go away, but he never explained the reasons why. When I realised he was gone I wept, for I knew it was too short a while that I knew him. In that short time I loved him, and I realised that no-one could ever replace him. To me he was a special man.

The Mooneys treated me as one of their own. May was a lovely person, as was Lorcan. I got on famously with him, even though I often disturbed his sleep. We never had a lot of money, but what we had we got great value for. I loved Dublin as a city. Being an ex-Artaner I suppose it was like being part of a great fair; it was smashing to walk home from the ballrooms without any fear of trouble. Dublin was a lovely place then. I hated going home too early in case I'd miss out on something, as I found the city at night to be a terrific place to be in.

4

What an Explosion!

I hadn't changed much as far as I could see in the one year since I had left Artane. It was about this time that I qualified with my old dance partner for the grand final of the Mícheál O'Hehir Cup, to be held in the Irish Club in Parnell Square. I recall Lorcan Mooney asking me what I did when I was with girls. 'Well,' I responded, 'I love their company. I enjoy dancing and talking to them.' Lorcan was quick off the mark. 'Is that all you do, Pat?' I looked at him with some amusement and replied, 'That's all. What else is there?'

Minnie Kelly came to visit me at the bakery one day. I was very surprised to see him. He had grown taller; he looked like a real gentleman! We walked into the city, to the Palm Grove in O'Connell Street. The stories Minnie told me filled me with sadness. He was a trained cook and baker. In Artane when I worked in the boys' refectory with him we were known as the kitcheners. Later I worked with him in the bakery, and he had moved on to work in the Brothers' refectory. Minnie was sent away to Salthill in Galway to a hotel, and then on to some farm as a houseboy. There he was very badly treated and abused, like so many other Artane boys, who were so naïve and had no-one to look to for help. I was lucky in that way: I was well treated by Mick and Pauline Bradley.

By the end of March a new baker had joined us. He was a

rare one. His name was Mark, but he was known to us as Mando. He was tall, very dark in complexion, with deep dark-blue eyes and a round handsome face. He was a slick talker and gentle mover. Mando was a superb and elegant ballroom dancer. At that time we had a midnight start in the bakery, and I often came from a dance and went straight in to work.

I had got to know the people around Fairview and I was known in most if not all of the shops, especially those along Fairview Strand. The fruit and vegetable shop was run by Mr Warren, and next door to him were Jim and Peggy Behan, who had just moved in. Beside them was, and still is, Hogan's pharmacy. All these people lived at their premises, at the rear or upstairs. The snooker hall, which stands as good as ever, still backs on to the side of the bakery grounds and old house. Little has changed since, except that people have passed on.

April 1959 I can never forget, for a number of reasons. One was that I was in the old-time waltz final. My partner and I were quietly confident of bringing home the cup. On the night of the final the Irish Club was packed to capacity and the atmosphere was electric. My partner, who was training to be a nurse in the Mater Hospital, brought fifty screaming nurses with her. I believed we were going to win as the adjudicators moved about, casually eliminating couples. Finally it was down to the last six. I looked at my partner, who I had been dating just for dancing pleasure. In fact at that time I had not actually dated a girl. I don't recall having had that kind of interest, and I never had the urge to go any further than taking one step forward or two steps sideways. Yet I loved being in the company of girls, just for their companionship.

For the second-last heat of the final there was much more room to dance, so to the cheers of the crowd I decided to take the floor by storm and walk away with the cup. My partner commented, 'It's between just a few of us now. It's in our grasp, Pat. My friends from the Mater will cheer us on.' I had never kissed a girl, and by gosh how I wanted to kiss her now! I went to do it and had just got there when the MC gave the word to begin dancing.

To the cheers of her friends from the Mater, I put in some fancy footwork that Mando had taught me during our breaks. My partner and I were being cheered on by a chorus shouting our names, and I was about to say 'well done' to her when the music stopped. The céilí band fell silent on the completion of 'The Northern Lights of Old Aberdeen'. As my number was called out by the MC, the excited crowd cheered.

I moved forward to caress my partner when suddenly the MC announced that number 7 was eliminated, to the sound of fierce booing and catcalls. I stood there silently watching another couple collect the cup. Before I could gather my thoughts I realised that not only had I not won the coveted cup but I had also lost my fabulous dance partner. She slipped away into the crowd. I can only imagine how the poor girl felt.

The night to follow was to be a long and famous one. I had to dash straight to work. It was Eddie's night off, which never seemed to work out for us. Everything would go wrong.

One of the special virtues I learnt in school was always to be on time, that it was far better to arrive half an hour early for work or for an appointment than to come a few minutes late. I have followed that code all my life, and I'm not at all happy with people who turn up late for engagements.

I got off the bus in Fairview at Edge's Corner and I hurried up Windsor Avenue towards the bakery. As I entered the yard of the bakery the church bell sounded. I closed the gate and smiled, and muttered, 'I made it on time.' I noticed that the bakery lights were on as I entered, but I found myself alone. It was midnight. My instinct told me to check the ovens to see if Mando had forgotten to light them. There were two gas ovens, each of them with five decks. One of them the boss bought from Woolworth's bakery in Henry

Street in 1957. I noticed that the taps were full on. I could see the light, so I decided to get changed.

As I began to leave, Mando walked in, his whites on and ready for work, but we'd be late starting because the ovens had only been put on. Mando checked the ovens once more and asked me to get a light and the supper.

I began to leave when he shouted, 'Paddy, get me the usual,' which was a one-and-one. I wasn't there till I was back, and Mando had the tea brewing on the open gas ring on the floor. I could smell the hot-plates heating up, but wondered about the ovens. I got the impression that something was wrong, and so did Mando. As he opened up the fish supper he shouted at me to check the ovens. I knelt down to check the lower deck, as from there I could see the jets and it was there I put the light in. I shouted to Mando, 'They're out.'

After getting the box of matches, I glanced towards Mando, who was now sitting up on the table enjoying his chips. I bent down. I noticed that some jets were out, but I wasn't thinking of anything other than lighting them to get on with the work. I don't recall getting a strong smell of gas as I bent down and struck the match.

What an explosion! As I lifted my head up, the top metal door of the first deck blew over my head, and a ball of fire swept across the ceiling and scorched my hair. As I stooped down to get out of the fire the lower deck blew its door off, bashing my right hand. I ran out, screaming for help. I couldn't see Mando, but I remember the final explosion as I stood or sat behind an evergreen bush in the front garden. A huge flame rose from the roof, and the windows blew out. As the ovens went up I could see a cloud of dust rise in Mr Warren's back yard. I'll never forget Mando's words as he stood in the front yard facing me. 'Me shaggin' supper! I was havin' me feckin' fish and chips, Paddy!'

I tried to laugh but I couldn't force it out, as my hand was too painful and I was in shock. I remember saying to him, 'Go and do something to put out the fire.' He looked at me with a big grin on his handsome face and remarked dryly, 'I could do with a week or two off, Paddy.'

I staggered round to Mr Warren's shop. A crowd had gathered, wanting to see what had blown up. I was surrounded now. I could hear the bells of the approaching fire engines and was aware of flashing lights.

A man came out holding a glass. I heard his voice and recognised it as that of Mr Brennan, the friendly grocer. 'Drink this, me lad, quickly.' I was in another world, never thinking at all what was in the glass. Mr Brennan shouted again, as though I had been deafened by the explosion. I put the glass to my lips. I saw the golden glitter of the liquid as I gulped it down. 'It'll do yeh good,' a man shouted. 'Sure it'll do yeh no harm anyway,' said another. My eyes popped. The last thing I remember was Mr Warren asking, 'What'yeh give him, Bill?' 'Glass o' brandy.' I was on my back on the pavement, looking up at the starry sky. The world was going round and round as I was lifted onto a stretcher and driven away at speed to Jervis Street Hospital.

The next day I was back in business, my forehead bandaged and right hand strapped up. I was standing in the bakery and looking out at the posse of policemen in the garden, searching for clues. I looked at Mando and we suddenly burst into laughter. The only clues I could see them finding were what Mando and I were to have had for our supper.

I was given a few days off. It was Friday and the men had hoped to get the bakery back in shape by Monday, to the dismay and annoyance of poor Mando. We began to move away from the bakery, to get out of the way of the gas workers—who had been blamed for causing the explosion, as they had been working on the mains up Windsor Avenue at the time. Suddenly Mando surprised me by saying, 'I need new lodgings in a hurry, Paddy. I believe you're well got in Fairview.' I smiled at him, not realising what sort of chap he really was, hiding behind his dark and handsome features. I found him lodgings with my new landlady, Miss Cashin, who ran a small grocery shop beside Mulvey's, the butchers, in Fairview

Strand. I had left the Mooneys with much regret soon after Bill Mooney had gone away.

My only fear after the explosion was that I wouldn't be able to travel to Navan with the great Leitrim footballer Frank Quinn and the lads for the National Football League semi-final between Dublin and Cavan. John Timmons and Frank Quinn were friends of the Cashins, and I recall many a Dublin footballer being in the house facing the park for tea. Dublin were indeed firm favourites to beat the Cavan men— just as I was the favourite to win the cup a few nights before!

5

My First Date

When I look back on my past, 1959 brings happy memories. It was an eventful year.

I was settling in to my new lodgings in 3 Fairview Strand with the Cashin family, who made me feel very welcome. This gave me a smashing feeling; I was really in my element with them. I was one of at least four lodgers in the house, which was fronted by a small grocer's shop, and beside it was Mulvey's butchers. Bridie Cashin ran the grocery shop. Sometimes I was asked to help out; the only problem was that I could never look straight at a customer, as I would get into fits of laughter at the size, shape or appearance of them—a throwback to my Artane days, when a new Brother was given a nickname within his first half-hour of duty. This was a real problem I had, and I was trying to change, as Mick Bradley had advised.

There was no shortage of things to do after work or at the weekends. Though there was no such thing as television or videos, I was never at a loss. Whatever was there we made terrific use of it. In one corner of the large sitting-room rested the old gramophone, which I fondly wound up by hand, and I sat back by the open turf fire at night listening to songs our fathers loved: 'The Rocks of Bawn', 'The Bold Fenian Men', 'Boolavogue', and 'The Rising of the Moon'.

I never felt alone in Bridie's place: there was a warm

welcome waiting for everyone. It wasn't unusual for me to get into my single bed in the room I shared with two other lodgers only to waken up to find I was sharing my bed with some tall GAA county footballer, one of many such visitors to the Cashins' place, which was a real Tipperary house.

I have fond memories of card games that went on into the night while the seventy-eights on the gramophone kept the spirits high. I found great peace and joy just to sit and watch those men, all so contented together. There was no money to be won or lost, just good crack by the turf fire.

One night I heard a loud tapping on the window, everyone else being preoccupied with the cards in their possession. I answered the door; and standing before me, almost breathless, was a very attractive young woman. 'I'm Isabelle,' she said. I was overwhelmed by her. How I wanted to touch her, to feel her beautiful skin! Her lips looked so tempting. She was a few years older than me. She spoke again. 'Could you tell Terry I'm here? I hope I can stay the night. Is Bridie at home by any chance?' I could have fallen for her there and then. I smiled and said, 'I'll go and tell them you're here. They're playing cards.'

For the first time I experienced a sensual feeling for the opposite sex, and I loved it. As I sat down by the fire I couldn't take my eyes off Isabelle. What I'd give to have her take care of me! The thought never once occurred to me that I had no idea whatever about sexual matters or women. The more I studied Isabelle and Terry as they sat together by the fire facing me, the more I wanted to be in Terry's place. As I watched them I began to realise there was something missing in my life. Though I had no idea how to go about it, I began to feel I was spending far too much time with ex-Artaners rather than with girls. I wanted to be with someone like Isabelle.

I was over seventeen and had never been out with a girl. Though I was really keen to try it out, I hadn't a clue how to go about it.

At the time of my first date I was earning £3 7s 6d a week

and I was paying Bridie Cashin £1 15s for full board plus my laundry. It was May 1959. I found myself in the happy position of being in the money, and I believed I could afford to chance going out with a girl, as Bridie often encouraged me to do. I was saving hard to go to the Isle of Man for a week's holiday, but I hadn't yet told my boss or the lads in the bakery. I had decided to take my holidays in June and see the famous TT races while I was there.

Dancing was still my favourite pastime, and I loved the old-time waltz. One evening while glancing through the evening paper I noticed a competition being run in the Irish Club. I decided at once I was going. When I arrived I noticed a young, slim, fair-haired girl standing chatting to her friend. The hall was quite empty, and as I approached her a chap got in ahead of me. I paused, and I was glad when I saw that he took her friend up to dance. She turned to me with a really suggestive smile. I knew then, at that instant. Our eyes met; our smiles kissed. That evening I danced in the arms of someone I had longed and yearned for.

The competition was going well; we reached the quarter-finals. I'll never forget the great Gallowglass Céilí Band. They filled the air with their wonderful sound. I waltzed that night into the arms of love. I didn't have to ask her for a date, or if I could see her home. It was altogether different. We simply went together up the steps at the rear of the bandstand and had our Club Orange, eying each other, nice and easy. What amazed me about it was how simple it all was.

Noeleen was at least five feet six and slim, with blue eyes. Her fair hair was short and permed. She was nearly two years older than me, and she came from Drumcondra. With a little hindsight I'm certain if I had known just a little about sexual matters it would have worked out, as Noeleen was a joy to be with.

We left the ballroom together, though I felt I was following her, and wherever she chose to stop suited me fine. Whatever moves she made were new to me. I loved it, and was quite happy to go along with her, as I was on cloud nine.

We went for a lemonade and a chocolate queen cake to the small grocery shop opposite the cinema at the corner of Dorset Street; it was a regular haunt for couples who went to the Teachers' Club or Granby Hall and the Irish Club. She walked into the laneway between the two blocks. We were standing in an old doorway, and as I looked across I could see the fluorescent lighting over the ballroom further along in Granby Lane.

But I couldn't come to terms with Noeleen in the way she expected. She was without doubt the leading player. I was nervous, to say the least. My arm rested around her shoulders. My hands were sweaty; I had to wipe them on her coat. Eventually I asked her about her last bus home. She smiled at me. Her blue eyes seemed to be pleading with me to caress her and to taste the sweetness of her breath and to touch her tantalising lips with mine, but I was so naïve, I didn't wish to commit a mortal sin. I was forever concerned about doing the right thing. 'You mustn't miss your bus,' I said.

Her hand took hold of mine and placed it inside her blouse on top of her breast. 'Never mind my bus, just feel my bust. See will you like it.' My body reacted with an unusual hunger, but I shook with fear of being seen. Then the sweat simply oozed from me. 'Glory be,' I moaned. 'I'm sure I've wet myself, or worse still, committed a dreadful act. Gosh, I've never felt like this before!' I was certain I had sinned, and felt sorry.

I made my first date with Noeleen that night as I walked her to the bus stop. She stood at the stop and spoke to me in a way no-one had ever spoken to me before. Her voice was sweet, soft as her body. 'Leave me home. I've a lovely place. You'll love it. There's a laneway and a long driveway up to my house. There are lots of bushes.' I felt out of my world, out of my depth, and as I look back, perhaps I was out of my mind. I was concerned for her well-being and that she get her last bus, as I felt responsible for her. 'Take me home, Pat.

You won't regret it.' Her lips pouted temptingly. She pulled me onto her. When our lips met I'm sure I wet myself.

As the bus arrived she almost devoured my mouth. I couldn't breathe. Oh God, I feared committing sin so soon again. 'I'll see you again, Pat. Perhaps the next time you'll see me home and go all the way.' Her smile was tempting. I wanted to pull her off the bus, but I was worried, as I was due in work at midnight with Mando and I knew he'd be mad if I was very late—though he thought little or nothing of being an hour or two late himself, or of not turning up at all.

Noeleen pulled open the window of the bus. She looked ravishing. 'I'll see you on Sunday night. Just say a place.' Without thinking I said, 'Outside the Fairview Grand.' She agreed. I hurried to get my bus to work, thrilled I had my first date.

Pretty Noeleen brought out in me many of my shortcomings, and she could see the dark side of my nature, which made me feel odd in her company. She decided in our short relationship that I was too naïve and not up to her special standards. I only had a few dates with her. The first could and should have ended the relationship. I booked two seats for the Fairview Grand for the Sunday night showing. When I looked back to that occasion years later I realised that I should have booked for the city, the Royal perhaps, as she lived in Drumcondra and I in Fairview. What's more, I loved and adored the big western films. I never really considered what Noeleen liked, and I have often said if I could have done things differently, I most certainly would have married my first date. It would have seemed so natural. In reality I was an emotional teenager, unable to see clearly.

As we entered the cinema I headed for the centre. She pulled me back; I wondered whatever for. She spoke quickly as the lights went low. 'Follow me,' she whispered, and we ended up sitting close to the wall at the back. I turned to her and asked her if she liked cowboy films. She whispered, 'No,' and smiled a very teasing smile, her lips almost on mine. She asked, 'Do you?' I responded at once. 'Of course. That's the reason I came.' She didn't answer. 'Do you like Errol Flynn?' I asked her. She smiled and shook her head. Suddenly she whispered, 'I like you a lot better. Are you really interested in all that horseshit?' I laughed. A voice from behind said, 'Shush. Shush, please.'

After a moment Noeleen whispered, 'Are you enjoying the film, Pat?' I was glued to what was going on along the Santa Fe Trail. I didn't even look at her but said, 'Yes, yes, I am, Noeleen.' 'That's too bad so,' she muttered and suddenly pulled my head towards her, to rest it on her breast. I was dumbfounded. Later her hand slowly crept below the flat of my stomach. For the first time in my life I felt sexually aroused. My lips were on her breasts. My eyes almost popped, and I made an odd sound. She looked me in the eye. 'Do you like what you see?' I was petrified. I couldn't think straight. Suddenly I got a tap on the shoulder and we were told to get out of the cinema at once. I followed Noeleen as the usher shone the torch on us all the way out.

I felt it was the beginning of the end, and it was a terrible moment for me. I was ashamed and felt I had let the Christian Brothers down. I never once thought of how Noeleen felt. The relationship never took off after that. However, it was an experience. It set me back quite a bit after I lost Noeleen; but there was far worse ahead. I knew I had no idea how to properly relate to girls like Noeleen, who expected me to react to her special needs. I believed I had to treat them all with great respect for fear of committing a sinful act, as I really did believe all my religious teaching.

I was only too aware of the fact that I was a great talker, but girls like Noeleen were not really interested in talk, or in cowboy films. Noeleen was a nice girl to chat to. She spoke well and I liked to listen to her. She was a rare one, though slightly ahead in years and far too experienced for me. She came upon me like a breath of fresh air. I was amazed by her actions and sexy suggestions, which left me with strange feelings that I enjoyed, though at the time I was ever fearful of doing wrong. I never seemed to catch on to the fact that it was Noeleen's way of saying 'I love you.' I never copped on that I was supposed to do the same and to please her in that way. I could only ever look at the wrongs and the rights of what she was doing, although I loved it. I believed I was committing acts of mortal sin in going along with her.

I was certain I was in love with Noeleen, and I seemed to fall in love with every girl that went out with me after that.

6

The Isle of Man

As June approached, there was only one thing on my mind: my holiday, which I had saved very hard for.

At that time I was taking stick from everyone and for anything that went wrong in the bakery. Mando was the funny man with the dancing feet, and a smooth talker if ever there was one. He would simply borrow or beg to get any money he needed. He knew, as did others, that I had money saved. Mando would and did pawn the suit off his back, and anyone else's as well.

Mando was a slick mover. I found myself almost trapped in his company during 1959. He was in lodgings in the same house as me. I found working with him good fun, but being in the same house was a bit too much. I believed and hoped he would leave.

On the first day he stayed in Cashins there were four lodgers at the table when the soup was served. Mando didn't think much of the soup, and while Miss Cashin was out in the kitchen he hurried up to the toilet with it, quickly flushed it away, and returned to join us. Miss Cashin came in to enquire if we had enjoyed the soup. Mando was first to answer: 'It was beautiful, ma'am,' and gave her a winning smile. I will always remember the look on his face when Bridie responded swiftly and poured him out a second helping of the soup. He never got the chance to flush it either.

Mando and our new van driver, the Jap Regan, were after the money I had saved to go to the Isle of Man. When Mick Bradley heard I was going by boat to the island he quickly offered to pay the air fare for me. I accepted, and was delighted. When the Jap heard, he moved quickly to borrow fifteen pounds from me, and offered to drive me to the airport. What amazed me at the time was that men who were so mature and settled—some were married and had nice homes to go to after work—were begging and borrowing whatever money I had worked so hard to save. I never received any money back, as they had promised.

Carmella O'Grady told me many times when I visited her that I should never lend money to a friend for any reason; if they were really so stuck or hard up I should simply give them a few pounds and tell them to keep it. Carmella believed that if I did that they wouldn't come looking for money from me again. She believed that eaten cake was quickly forgotten. I fully agreed, but not until it was too late.

I have fond memories of my first trip out of Ireland. It was a Friday, and I was to meet the Jap in the bakery at four. My flight was shortly after five.

The Jap was out delivering the buttermilk bread. At a quarter to five he drove into the yard shouting, 'Pat, Pat, damn it, are you ready? I'll get you there if I have to drive out to meet the plane.' I threw my case into the back of the van among the sodas. We were away in a flash as he scraped the pillar going through the front gates. When we reached the Swords road I was scared stiff. He swerved by lorry and bus, weaving from lane to lane, until eventually we got to the airport. I had been very apprehensive of flying, but as I got out of the battered van, covered in flour dust, all the tension I had previously built up had disappeared, so that my first flight was most enjoyable.

I fell in love with the Isle of Man the first moment I set foot on its soil. It reminded me of a paradise island in the sun that I had seen in the school cinema. I was overwhelmed by its beauty, its gardens, and most of all its beautiful glens. The names of Glen Mona, Glen Myra and Laxey Glen bring back fond and cherished memories.

I went alone to the island, but once there I seemed to find company without really looking for it. Perhaps it found me. I entered a waltz competition, and I had an English partner, from Redcar in the north of England. We did well on the dance floor, and I still treasure the photographs of the occasion. She was a good few years older than me, but nevertheless I dated her, and it all helped me to enjoy the wonderful island. I sat in my room in the guesthouse, thinking that the English people were really human after all!

One breathtaking evening I was making my way up the steep climb known as Darby Hill when a young woman came alongside me, rather breathless. 'Have you the time, please?' I stopped, glanced at the cheap watch I had treated myself to an hour previously, gave her the time, and thought nothing of it. A few moments later, nearer the brow of the hill, I heard her voice. As I turned to see who it was, she was upon me. 'Hey, Irish, we're going the same way. Mind if I walk with you?' Her smile was oozing with warmth as the evening sun kissed her long golden hair. 'Call me Pat,' I said, and added, 'I'll be delighted to walk with you.'

She smiled, almost laughed, and said, 'Blimey, you really are sweet.' 'Well, I'm not a stage Irishman, you know. I'm just me.' She stroked back her hair and said, 'Call me Gloria. I come from Redcar, in England.' I was curious. 'Have you an older sister here?' She faced me and said, 'Yes, I have. She's in the dance championships.' So that's her, I thought, and smiled.

I followed her through an opening to the park. The roses were in full bloom. We stood close, admiring them. I longed to touch her, and then without warning or planning we embraced. Her lips met mine in a wave of passion. Her hands gripped tightly around my waist. Mine went even further and found a trail beneath her light, colourful summer skirt, only to tear through her even lighter panties. 'Oh, gosh!' I cried out. 'I'm so sorry!' She smiled softly and said,

'It's all right, there's no problem.' I felt awfully embarrassed though. She noticed.

As we walked I felt terrible for having got carried away. She looked at me. 'You're still blushing. I can tell you're not used to going with girls. You're so nervous and over-anxious. You shouldn't make a fuss over things you do like that; it really is fine, you know.' She smiled and added, 'It's all part of the fun, you know.'

She paused, and smiled temptingly. I wanted to try it again. My old ex-Artane undies wouldn't give way so easily, I thought. 'What are you thinking, Irish? Your smile suggests something very sexy. Want to tell me?' How could I, I thought, and eased my hands around her until our lips met in a heavenly movement. After a long moment she whispered, 'Take care, Pat. You don't know your own strength.' We laughed together as we meandered through the gardens and back to her guesthouse. My heart raced. I had to see her again. I longed for the touch of her body. 'Can I see you again, perhaps tomorrow?' I waited anxiously. 'I'm so sorry, Irish—sorry, Pat, but I'm going home in the morning. If only we met a week ago!' I walked away haunted by Gloria's last words. If only ...

I began to fall in love with any girl who went out with me, yet I knew absolutely nothing about sexual intercourse. I began to find myself in the company of girls quite a lot, some of whom were most attractive and pleasant to be with. I found to my utter disappointment that it was the girls I liked and loved the most that I couldn't have. I knew then for certain that I was doing something wrong—or perhaps it was the fact that I was doing nothing that was the problem, as was the case with beautiful Noeleen.

Near the end of my holiday I met a Liverpool girl by accident. She was working in the Grand Cinema, and for some reason she asked me to hold her torch as she helped someone out. I watched as the cinema became empty. When she finally returned we were alone. The lights dimmed and we sat in the back row chatting. She made all the moves, some of which amazed me. I soon dropped her torch, while her smooth hands went to work on me. As I gulped and ooched, I wondered what on earth this girl wanted. I didn't even get her name, though we had been chatting for some time. Her accent was very Liverpudlian—so strange to me, but I liked it. We walked together from the Grand, yet I seemed to be following her. When we came to the tram terminus we both stood watching the horses getting a rub-down.

I was more out of touch, again out of my depth as I walked and talked to this Liverpool lass. She had long sandy hair, water-blue eyes, and a pointed chin with a small dimple. She was about five feet six inches in height and her voice was chirpy. I loved it. I was inspired and passionately encouraged by her hunger and sexual enthusiasm. 'To hell with the Devil and committing mortal sin,' I thought. I felt wild and free to let her do as she pleased. It never occurred to me that I was to satisfy her needs, or perhaps it was that I didn't know how.

We came to rest on a green sloping bank. There she spoke about the sea and about England. It was a calm, sultry night. It was the night I almost lost my manhood and virginity all at once. As she talked about the Mersey, Liverpool and Birkenhead, she almost tore me apart. She wore a ring on almost every finger. One of them was quite a size and sharp; it caught me as I was never caught before, and how I screamed! Suddenly I began rolling down the cliff, shouting for help, while my trousers hung around my ankles. She came good, though, my Liverpool lass, and saved me from falling into the calm blue water a few hundred feet below.

She looked at me rather apologetically, I thought, and said, 'I like you, Paddy, but I could never stay a night with you. You have no action.' I felt deflated. Then she added dryly, 'You're so different. You do nothing, do yeh, except stare at me as though I was some sort of untouchable goddess.'

She looked me in the eye as we stood on top of the cliff. 'Ta-ra, mate. See yeh.' I looked at her as she breezed away into the warm night, strolling along the Cliff Road down to

Douglas. I realised something was wrong but I simply couldn't work out what it was. If only Mando was here, I thought. He'd know the ropes!

As she disappeared from view, I gulped, swallowed my pride, and muttered, 'Never again!'

I toured the beautiful island from Douglas to Port Erin, the Russian Abbey, and the grave of 'Some Mother's Son'. I went back to work in the Isle of Man in 1961, and returned on many occasions to holiday there with my family. That first trip away from Ireland gave me a window to the world at large. It opened up my closed mind and encouraged me to travel on and go much further.

7
Liverpool and London

In 1960 I was not getting anywhere in the bakery. I was losing my girl-friends as fast as I could find them.

In the lodgings I was sharing with Mando I was spotlessly clean—always dusting, polishing, and tidying up things that were out of place, forever putting things back and hanging up coats. I never liked men who simply entered a house in their working clothes, threw their gear and clothes on chairs, and put their feet up near the fire so everyone could smell their smelly feet! I was very domesticated.

Mando was now the foreman of the small bakery, and I was his deputy. But it was not doing at all well. I realised that to get on I'd have to go abroad. I was becoming ambitious, and I was no longer prepared to remain on low wages for ever. I was working all sorts of hours, which were very unsociable, and I began to get a burning desire to travel.

Mando owed over a month's rent. One evening I came back from playing a match and noticed that he was packing. He believed there was no-one about. Miss Cashin's brother, Mick, was standing up on the window ledge cleaning the front window. Mando called me to his room. I wasted no time in seeing what he wanted me for. 'Hello, Mando, I'm here. Have you got a problem?' He eyed me with those big dark eyes of his and said, 'Look, Paddy, I'm moving on. I've got to get out now. I need you to check down at the shop. If anyone starts to come up or even ask for me, I'm out.' 'But you're here,' I said. 'And what's more, how are you going to slip out past the shop?' He grinned at me slyly. 'You keep watching the front and you'll see me wave to you. That means I'm in the clear. Okay, Paddy? Are you with me?'

I casually looked out the door, thinking that Mick would have the window finished, but I was shocked to see a suitcase pass over him and land on the pavement. In a flash Mando was down onto it, whipping it up. Mick, realising what Mando was doing, took possession of the case, and Mando fled, swearing back at him.

Mick came towards me with a surprised look on his handsome face, muttering, 'All that for the sake of a few quid in rent, Paddy!' Putting down the case, he wiped his forehead and said, 'It wouldn't happen in my home town in Tipperary.'

Things were getting bad in the bakery. Mando came up with a plan of action, and I was to be a key player. He had told me on so many occasions how he knew England well and how he had picked fruit in the great gardens of England. He wanted me to travel to Liverpool with him—a giant step for me to take—but I also knew that Mando was a chancer. He told me that if I didn't like Liverpool he'd have me back without a bother. His plan was that he would take a week's sick leave and that I was to take a week off to simply try it. If it didn't work, he promised he'd have me home and at work in a week.

On the boat journey to Holyhead I listened to the playing of traditional music, as there were many fine young musicians and buskers on board that night. I watched many people with tears in their eyes, seated uncomfortably on the floor or on suitcases. By the time I got onto the train I felt as though I had already been away for a week.

Mando knew all the ropes. I stood in the employment exchange with him. He had briefed me on how to answer their questions. As it worked out, I was given twice as much money as he was. We were both sent to a big bakery outside the city; after a few days we were both given a sub—an advance on our wages. At last I had some real cash.

The house where we stayed was in a very run-down and dangerous area. Mando suddenly began to take a deeper interest in my well-being but, as always, with strings attached. He wanted my money for safe keeping. Well, my memory was not that short. I knew my money was safer where it was—in my shoes.

One night Mando decided to retire to bed early. I was sitting up, listening to his advice and his new plans. He began to tell me about women and sexual matters, when suddenly the door burst open and two black men stood in front of us. I froze to my chair. I almost wet myself, or perhaps I did. Mando jumped out of bed and realised that he was naked and his clothes were on a chair near the two intruders. The silence was broken when both of them roared with laughter, pointing at Mando. Suddenly Mando shouted at me to give them something. Without even thinking, I took Mando's coat, which was next to me on a chair, and said, 'You want it? Please take it and leave us alone. We won't harm you.' I was scared stiff but decided to join them in their laughter. Suddenly one of them came towards me and put out his hand. 'Shake, Irish. You're fun! You sure are some fun guy, I tell you.' I never took my eyes from him. I shook his hand and watched as the other chap moved towards Mando, who seemed to be frozen to the floor in the nude. Mando was suddenly being hugged by the guy. While he did all he could to cover himself up, the men hurried away.

It must have been four or five in the morning when I jumped out of the old double bed I shared with him. I was burning with a dreadful itch. I turned on the light and was horrified to see my body covered with bites and awful-looking lumps. I watched as Mando woke up shouting, 'Put off the fuckin' light, for fuck's sake!' Mando got out of bed that morning almost tearing at his flesh. 'I'm flea-bitten, for Christ's sake!' He was swearing like a raving lunatic now, and then he noticed that I was in an even worse state than himself.

I stood naked in a cubicle with two very attractive English nurses attending to me. It was the first time, I believe, I had to take my clothes off for a woman. Mando refused to come in with me and preferred to wait for me outside. One of the nurses was watching Mando while she attended to me. She spoke with a refreshingly soft voice, which was very English. 'Is he with you, then?' I smiled at her and nodded yes. 'Oh, gosh, he is cute, Georgina, isn't he then?' I was being soaked in lotion all over my body. Both of them got very interested in Mando. 'Cor! He's so dark and tall and so cute too.' They were both in agreement, and suddenly they called him in. Mando looked worried as he stood gazing at me, naked and covered in pink lotion. One of the nurses quickly asked Mando, 'What about you, then? You've been bitten too, then?' Well, I never saw Mando move as quickly as he did at that moment.

It was our fifth day in Liverpool. Mando had had enough of the filthy lodgings, and I had told him I would rather get on the boat than remain one more night. I arranged to meet him in Lime Street Station, as he gave me a story about a business matter he had to attend to. He advised me to get on the London train before it was due to pull out if he didn't catch up with me. He would be on the train either way, he assured me.

Well, I should have known Mando. I only realised where he disappeared to six months later, when I eventually returned to Dublin after an incredible experience in London on my first night. What I'd have given to have had Mando with me then!

THE TRAIN JOURNEY from Liverpool to London seemed like a week. I wasn't to know that ahead lay the most awful night I've ever known. Alone in a compartment, I sat gathering my thoughts. 'Where will I sleep tonight?' I kept asking myself. At intervals I'd steal a few moments to close my eyes and think back on my Ireland and how fond I was of sitting in a smoke-filled room in Cashin's in Fairview, listening to songs of Ireland—songs that never failed to fill my heart with pride.

As the train eased into the station, I began to feel that I had again been deserted. Now for the first time in my life I was completely alone. I actually felt stripped naked as I walked up the platform. In the suitcase Carmella O'Grady had given me some months before for my holiday in the Isle of Man lay all my worldly belongings. 'Good God,' I thought, 'will I ever see Ireland again?' Then I heard the loud but sweet chimes of Big Ben telling the city of London it was midnight. 'God,' I asked, 'what lies ahead of me here?'

I put down my suitcase on the pavement outside the station. I gazed around and saw the row of taxis, flashing lights, people hurrying, all hustle and bustle. I gazed along a row of guesthouses; *No vacancies* the signs all read. The awful feeling of lonely emptiness got hold of me. I was full of self-pity. I began to pray to Jesus, then to Mary and St Joseph.

I heard a voice in front of me, and as I looked up I could clearly see the man's round, fat face. His neat dark hair, though it was tightly cut, suited his strong, heavy build. He looks very posh, and a nice fancy suit too, I thought. His voice was smooth. 'You waiting for someone, mate?' I muttered to him, 'I'm alone—I lost my friend Mando in Liverpool—Lime Street.' He sounded very sympathetic. 'You're Irish and you've no place to stay. I'll put you up for the night and see you're okay in the morning. How's that, then, Paddy? I hope you don't take no offence, calling you Paddy, then, do you?' I responded at once with hope in my heart. I smiled. I got swiftly into his car, and within minutes I was in his flat.

I found myself standing in very strange surroundings. My mind went more or less blank for a short while as I stood gazing about. Only when he returned to offer me something to eat did I begin to feel myself. The lighting in the apartment was very seducing. It instantly caught my attention as he calmly showed me around. There was one sitting-room cum dining-room, a very well-decorated bathroom with shower, a small kitchen, and one good-sized bedroom.

I felt tired as I stood looking at the large double bed with its neat matching lockers on each side, and red velvet shades, which gave the room a warm glow. I had never seen such comforts before. Comfort to my mind meant the lodgings in Fairview, sitting by a log and turf fire with the Cashins and friends, listening to Din Joe and songs and ballads on the radio. Such thoughts while I was away from Ireland instantly brought feelings of sadness and tears of love for my beloved Ireland. What's going to happen now? I wondered.

'Would you like some supper, Paddy?' I felt relieved. I hadn't eaten since I left Mando at least eight hours before. I smiled and accepted, with delight showing on my face. 'Do you like toast and tea, Paddy?' Do I what! I wasted no time in saying, 'Yes, sir' excitedly. He shouted now as he was out in the kitchen. 'Call me Melvin. My mates call me Mel at times.' I was now seated on the bed, getting the feel of it. Suddenly he called out to me to get into bed and he would serve me supper. It never dawned on me for a moment what lay ahead.

I began to undress. Then I remembered that my clothes were in the case, and I knew I'd feel awkward in bed in the nude. As he appeared in front of me, holding a tray containing supper, I instantly dived into bed and covered myself. I was wearing only my underpants, and they were awful-looking ones at that!

Melvin looked down at me. His voice was soft but deep. It suited the atmosphere, I thought. 'You enjoying your bit of supper, Paddy? I'm sorry, it's all I've got in at the moment. I like tea and toast before I go to bed, mind you.' He began to undress, and as I finished my toast I began to study him. I was amazed as he sprayed his body and I got the whiff of body cologne. I noticed him putting on hair cream, then he turned and got into bed beside me. He placed the service tray in front of us. It was then I noticed its full contents: hot buttered toast, strawberry jam, tea, and Vaseline. It never dawned on me to ask what the Vaseline was for.

I got a strange feeling through my body, and for the first time since he picked me up at the station I was worried. Quickly I turned on my side and brought my knees up. My bottom was suddenly against his body, and I could feel his body heat. I could hear the night sounds outside of a car passing. The silence inside was broken by the chimes of the beautiful old clock on the dresser. Without a word of warning I felt his hands on my body. Slowly first, then in a very soft voice, he spoke. 'I see you've got pants on.' I was fearful now as he eased them off. His hands were resting on my naked bottom. He whispered words of comfort. I was too frightened to move or to answer him. I knew now this was to be a night to remember—providing I got out alive, that is.

I was now fully aware of my predicament, and it struck me that no-one in the world knew of my whereabouts. Suddenly I was to learn with horror what the Vaseline was for. I hadn't moved an inch from the way I had chosen since he got in beside me, as I lay in fear of the unknown.

The clock chimed once, leaving a quaint ring like an echo. I began to pray for help to the Lord Jesus for strength and faith to pull me through as I could feel his hands spreading thick Vaseline over my buttocks and back passage. I could feel the coldness of the Vaseline and his big warm hand massaging my private parts and buttocks. I was now in a cold sweat and ready to jump out of bed, yet too frightened to do so. I asked myself while he continued his massage, 'Where do I run to?' I couldn't fight Melvin. He was far too heavy and strong for me to handle. I wondered what lay ahead; I hadn't long to wait. He began to chat to me; his breathing became heavy now. Suddenly his tone changed. 'I'm not going to hurt you now, I promise you.' I began to cry out loud as he attempted to penetrate me. I could feel the pain—it was too much. I screamed out as he tried desperately to enter me, but I knew I had put him off. Through fear and the knowledge that what he was attempting to do was wrong, I struggled and cried out for him to stop, and I thanked the Lord that he calmed down and backed off, though he was still holding on to my bottom and private parts while he moaned to me.

Melvin realised now that whatever he was seeking from me he could not have, or he most certainly could not have in comfort or with enjoyment. He spoke to me for a few moments. 'I'm sorry if I hurt you and sorry for putting you through this ordeal on your first night in London.' I remained silent. 'I notice, Paddy, you're different. You seem to be well brought up. I've met a lot of Irish lads as they arrive here—lost, no place to stay, and they're glad to come to my place and stay for a few weeks. I get some of them fixed up in night clubs and in photography with the boys.' I never uttered a word as he spoke his mind and tried to make me feel that what he was doing was all right.

I woke up next morning to the smell of roasted coffee, bacon, egg, and toast. I began to feel good again, no fears, and I trusted him to leave me somewhere safe. I prayed it wouldn't be at the bottom of the Thames.

What a relief I got when I stepped from his car in Piccadilly. Melvin wasted no time and sped away as soon as I closed the car door. I was alone again, but thanked God I was safe and no harm had come to me. Tears filled my eyes. I wondered what next, and I could have sworn at Mando and damned him for leaving me the way he did.

I noticed people in the street staring at me. I was also aware of the stalls on each side of the street, which instantly reminded me of the dealers in Moore Street. 'Christ,' I thought, 'I don't want to be picked up here.' I noticed magazines on a stand. The covers showed pictures in full colour of naked women! I was dumbfounded at such things, and as I stood outside a shop that was displaying sexual things and pictures of women in all sorts of positions, I became flushed. I decided to look for the nearest bakery, if there was one—or policeman. Whichever came first didn't matter to me.

'Hello, sir.' The London bobby stopped and responded quite nicely to me. 'Yes, lad, what's your problem?' I had to think quickly. 'I'm lost, sir, and hope you can help me. I'd like to join the police force if it's possible.' I was, of course, chancing my arm, and by doing so I hoped I'd get some sort of help and get out of the spot I found myself in. I was driven to a police station. It couldn't have been far from where I was, as I was only in the car a few minutes.

My height and weight were taken before I was informed that I wasn't tall enough—but they were a great help to me, as I had hoped they would be. I was dropped off at London's largest bakery, Lyon's of Cadby Hall, in Hammersmith. There I was offered a job on the spot and sent to a house in Kensington Road, where I was offered a room at the top, which I was pleased to accept without even seeing it.

It was an eight by ten foot bedsitter, and I had to share it with a young man from Glasnevin who worked for the BBC. What a relief! I sighed as I sat down on that bed, which was neat and clean, as was the room itself. God, I was so happy to have a room, a place I could call home and in a good clean house, with a terrific view of the city.

I worked six nights a week in Cadby Hall. I met a few ex-Artane lads, but my happiest moment was when I met Stephen Caulfield, who had lived in Barnacullia and been sent to Artane Industrial School shortly after myself. He was a nice, quiet lad. I met Stephen at a dance in the Emerald Ballroom in Hammersmith; he recognised me instantly. The first thing he told me was that he had found his parents and that he had three fine sisters. Well, I felt over the moon for Stephen. I have never met him since.

By December 1960 I was feeling very homesick for Ireland, not simply because Christmas was fast approaching but because the night work was getting me down. It was beginning to affect my health, and it was a relief to get up onto the flat roof during dinner break, about two in the morning. It made me feel better as I gulped the night air and gazed out across London on a clear night. I stood there with men from many parts of Ireland, including some ex-Artane lads who had been boy bakers at the age of fourteen, when they said Artane was a dangerous place to be in!

I met my old pal Oxo Ryan in Lyon's Bakery on the night shift, and he told me he had made his way to London after his last escape from Artane. As we sat in the bakery canteen night after night I listened to him reliving Artane. The thoughts of marching to Mass at twenty to seven every morning, through hail, rain, or snow at the age of eight, and on to breakfast for a quarter of a loaf of bread and an ounce of margarine with a mug of tea, was becoming a nightmare once more. I wondered if a time would ever come when I would be able to forget Artane.

Oxo Ryan's story had a profound effect on me. He told me how he had escaped from Artane and gone home, only to be brought back by his own mother! He was sent to the farm, which was like slavery. He escaped again, and on being returned again he was shaved bald and flogged until he bled. Then he was sent by Driller the Killer to the centre of the parade ground, where Driller ordered the crowd of older boys to attack him. I had remembered most of this myself.

'You know, Paddy, I couldn't shit for a week after the beatings, my arse was so cut up. But I wasn't going to be bested, and after six months of slavery and floggings I slipped away.' I could see by him and by the glint in his eyes that he won, but I got the feeling he missed his ma and longed to get home. 'The bastards never got me again. They taught us to hate England, but I love England, and what's more, the people here are more Christian than the Christian Brothers could ever be. Sure they don't go to bloomin' Mass every morning, but so what?' He laughed as he said that; I could see he enjoyed telling me all this.

I BEGAN TO feel poorly in late November. I knew it was the night work that was affecting not alone my eating habits but also my sleep. I could never get a really sound sleep while on night work. I was always so used to silence as a boy in Artane.

I would have remained in London if I had found someone I liked. In many ways I felt that travel gave me confidence,

By the sea in Blackrock, June 1969.

On the beach in Grave de Lee, Jersey.

Aged twenty on the sand of Grave de Lee, Jersey.

In hospital, Bradford Royal.

M.S. "SHOTA RUSTAVELI" 1970

In fancy dress aboard ship, 1970.

In Chile, 1970.

In New Zealand with Pa-Joe and Brigid.

Engagement photo with fiancée Pauline.

The wedding: bride and groom walking down the aisle.

The wedding: bride and groom at the car.

On honeymoon in El Arenal, Spain, February 1973.

though I was very much alone, as I was always on the move. I had my sights set on faraway places. The lads I met in London were all Irish, and they generally drank to get stone drunk. I didn't like pubs then, so perhaps that left me deprived somewhat, as I now believe the pub is a great place for making friends and meeting people.

One night in early December I was at work when I felt peculiar. I was working on a huge travelling oven when I suddenly collapsed. I was taken to hospital, where I was kept for ten days. The doctors told me to give up the night work, and the bakery trade also. 'If only I could,' I thought. While I was resting in hospital I had plenty of time to think of what I wanted to do. London had been a hell of an experience for me, which I could certainly have done without, but I was treated well at work and I earned plenty of money. But I was longing to be in Dublin for Christmas, in my own Ireland.

8

The Pawnshop

While I was in London I kept in touch with the Mooneys and the Cashins. I got a drop one day to learn that Bridie was moving shop from Fairview Strand to Macken Street, near Westland Row. 'Blast,' I thought. 'There goes another good lodging house for me.' As I turned over the page I was delighted to learn that I would be welcome home for Christmas if I could make it. Well, I made certain I would, and I never looked forward to Christmas as I did then.

I had saved most of the money I earned while I worked in Lyon's of Cadby Hall, and by the time Christmas came I had saved a few hundred. It was easy to earn good money then, and lodgings were cheap. I was working over sixty hours a week, at night, which left me with little time for enjoyment. I quickly realised that machines had taken over from the skills of the baker. All the good was taken away by the fact that anyone could get a job in Cadby Hall as mere machine operators, which I was.

I found it extremely difficult to book a flight to Dublin to be home in time for Christmas. I came out of hospital about the twentieth of December. All I was concerned about was getting back to Dublin; and I was blessed to get a standby fare on an early morning flight when some passenger failed to turn up.

I was determined to ride up in fine style by horse and carriage to the new shop, and looking back on that time I realise what kind of a dreamer I had turned out to be. As there was no room for me in Cashin's, I was to move once Christmas was over. It was the homeliest Christmas I've ever had. The Cashins were to me what love and warmth were all about. I began to realise that it would be hard for me to stay away from Ireland for any length of time.

I was back working in the buttermilk bakery that January. Eddie and Mando were also there. Eddie was about to leave to start a new bakery around the corner in Jim Behan's shop. Strange as it seemed to me, Jim Behan was the van driver for Mick Bradley and remained so for a while—I suppose until Eddie got the new venture off the ground. Stranger things still were to happen. Matt returned to work with us. I always thought it was difficult for an ex-Artane lad to make the grade—always returning to their roots or the humble beginnings from where they began on leaving Artane. I got to like Matt much more now and began finally to understand him and his ways.

Having heard at first hand Mando's explanation of how he lost me in Liverpool, I knew that whatever second thoughts I might have I'd certainly never travel anywhere again with him.

Once Mando organised a get-together for old time's sake. It was to the Rainbow Rooms in O'Connell Street; we were to meet him outside. He planned to go to his digs in Mountjoy Square first, and I travelled on the bus from Fairview with Eddie and Matt. Mando better be loaded to pay for the meals, I thought.

When we got to the café, Mando looked like an executive on a business trip. Matt and Eddie were almost as shy of approaching him as I was. Suddenly Matt couldn't stand much more of the gazing at each other and he broke the silence. 'Where'd yeh get the clobber, Mando—in the pawn office or from Dawson's dress hire in Paddy's name?' I watched Mando trying to explain as we went up the stairs.

As we sat around a table set for four by a window, I could

see down onto the busy pavement below and the tops of the double-decker buses, and at the same time I was listening to Mando explain how he came into money from a rich aunt who had died in London. I noticed Eddie shaking his head and laughing. Then Matt spoke, revealing so much about Mando. 'But I thought it was your mother who died, and she had no money whatsoever—didn't you borrow fifty quid to go over to her funeral last year?' The meal was being served when Eddie butted in. 'You owe me twenty quid, you know, for that trip, and you owe me for the trip to see your dying uncle in Manchester. How come you can afford to splash out on us now?' I watched carefully as Mando stood up and grinned at Matt. 'I'm going to the gents'—I'll explain it all to you. Order your desserts and one for me, and I'll finish off with a black coffee.' As he left I noticed a sly wink to me.

As I sipped my tea, for some reason or other I looked out the window. The tea suddenly poured down my nose and I splurted out with laughter. There was Mando on the pavement below.

I quickly looked at the lads enjoying a smoke. I stood up as the waiter came over to present the bill. 'I've got to go to the gents'.' I knocked over a chair in my rush to get past, and was noticed laughing by Matt—but I was ahead, and I knew I'd get out and down to Mando before they did. I almost fell down the stairs to get out. It was not my bill, and I could never have afforded it.

'What bleedin' kept you, Paddy? I thought you'd never cop on!' I glanced up at the window and there were Matt and Eddie and the waiter knocking and waving at Mando to come back. I followed Mando into town, and I simply put it all down to experience. As for the suit he wore, he produced the card with my surname: Edward Touher, c/o Bradley's Home Bakery, Fairview. He also had another union card with my name and another lad's address. He wore expensive suits, and pawned them all for what he was offered.

I travelled many times to the North Strand pawnshop. My first visit was with Mando, as was my last. On my first visit he took off his dark-blue Crombie overcoat and casually handed it across to the pawnbroker, who quickly examined the coat. 'It's new, this is,' he muttered. Mando looked and acted in a very confident manner. 'Fifteen pounds ten—I must have it: I've got to go to England to bury my aunt.' Good grief, I thought, another one! I smiled as I watched the pawnbroker count out twelve pounds and ten shillings and mutter, 'Such a fine coat. I hope when you return you'll be able to claim it back before the time runs out.' Mando looked so relieved. He gave me the impression he loved money more than anything. As we went to leave the pawnbroker said kindly, 'Sorry, lad, about your aunt, but I won't always be as generous.'

As far as I could see it was a speedy way of acquiring cash when one was desperate, but so many of the goods that were handed over to the pawnshop were not always honestly acquired. It was a strange sight to see men walk into a pawn office, neatly dressed, only to come out wearing a shirt and an old pair of trousers, also minus rings and watch—all for a few pounds in cash, for gambling, drinking, or smoking.

On one occasion Mando borrowed Eddie's bike, with a promise that he would have it back before Eddie finished playing Matt in a game of snooker around the corner from the bakery. Mando looked at me and gave me the nod to follow him. Once away from the bakery I soon realised what he was up to, as we cycled towards the North Strand. 'You're not going to pawn Eddie's bike now?' We stopped just short of the pawn office. He looked at me hard and said, 'Look, Paddy, you're me best mate. I need a tenner right now to pay the new landlady or I'll have no digs.' He pleaded with me. 'For feck's sake, Paddy, I brought you along as my pure witness, see. I'll tell Eddie the bike was nicked when we went in for a slash in Grainger's. When we came out the bike was gone—okay? I need this break, Paddy.' He had a sorrowful look. I agreed, providing he would take the bike out when he had the money.

The following week my own bike went missing. I checked

in the pawn office, and true enough, there it was. It cost me £2 17s 6d to take it out; I originally bought it for £3 15s from Mick Bradley.

9

Itchy Feet

How can I forget the 1960s—the dancing years! Those were the days when we got super value for our few shillings. I was earning only £3 15s and handing over £2 5s a week for full board. But I could afford to bring my girl-friend to the Theatre Royal for a stage show and a film, have supper afterwards in the Palm Grove and pay the bus fares, and still have change. I was rich when I got a fiver for Christmas or my birthday from Carmella O'Grady.

Showbands were in huge demand in the late 1950s and through the 1960s. Then, as people earned more money, the cost went up from five shillings for most ballrooms to ten shillings, or 50p, which was expensive. The showbands got bigger and better and the price rose to a pound or in the top ballrooms—which were all well outside the city, like the Top Hat and Laurel Park—to two pounds. The owners and the showbands killed off the goose that laid the golden egg.

The National and Ierne Ballrooms in Parnell Square were very much the haunts of the flat-dwellers from the country and of north city Dubliners. I moved my Thursday dance night from the Irish Club to the Ierne, because I felt I needed a change and to try dancing to modern music. I met a girl on my first visit.

Noreen was to be my first real love, and when we told each other our feelings after only a few dates together it was as though we should have simply gone off and got married. Noreen was eighteen, the same age as me, with long fair hair, blue eyes and slim build but with a sad face, suggesting that she might be lonely or homesick. I had only met her but I believed we were meant for each other, as we had a great deal in common. Noreen came from a good-sized family in County Cavan. She had five brothers and seven sisters—and all fine girls too!

I had a longing to travel, and I told May Mooney and Lorcan that I had a real desire to see the world. I looked at May, who was doing some ironing. I knew I had to have her sound advice. 'What do you think, May?' As she came to the end of the ironing she glanced at me and laughed. 'You don't need anyone's advice, Pat. You're too cute now for us. Any advice I'd give you, you'd simply go and do the opposite! For example,' she continued, as she became more serious, 'what about Noreen, the young girl you're going out with? She seems really a nice sort, and what's more, she's from the country.'

As I got up off my chair the cat, Oscar, hopped into my seat. May was quick off the mark. 'Even Oscar knows what he wants and takes it. Now you get out there to Noreen. You'll never leave Fairview Park, Pat.' I took the hint and decided to go for the only one who had ever said, 'I love you, Pat.'

As I look back now I believe it is a mistake to linger and become undecided about what to do. If a couple have accepted each other in a loving way, then it's decision time. I went out with Noreen for many months and decided that I couldn't afford to marry her then—I'd have to go abroad to earn a decent wage first. I loved Noreen. I simply knew nothing of sex. I doubt that she did either. Nevertheless, instead of steadfastly standing by her I got the boat to England like a fool.

I decided on my own that as I was not in a steady position that I liked—it was a dreadful source of bother to me that I was in night work and that I couldn't get a decent-paying non-union bakery job—I would leave Ireland but keep in touch with Noreen. It never crossed my mind to ask Noreen what she thought. I needed someone to control my thoughts and wild notions. Strangely, no-one did or offered to help me.

I suppose I didn't realise how Noreen really felt about me. I believed I was doing the right thing for the future. My wife often tells me now, whenever I speak of the future, 'Let the distant future look after itself. It's today we're living in, Pat.' Perhaps she's right. I believe it's wrong to put a love affair on ice, as I did—hoping to make a fortune somewhere and return to claim the girl you left behind, only to find her not there.

As 1961 approached I had a longing to write something. I began to write a radio script about a busker, and wrote songs to include in it. I never dreamed I needed to get it typed, and quickly sent it in to Radio Éireann. They sent it back, thanking me and telling me if I should write a further script to be sure to get it translated before sending it to them! They were joking, of course, but I got the message. It would be a long time before I'd try the same again.

I often felt so lonely and out of things that I actually began to believe I'd make a fine Christian Brother. One night I was preparing to go to Nulty Park House Golf Club, for the staff New Year party, when Lorcan Mooney, who was preparing also, looked at me. His tone was sincere and I could sense he meant what he asked, as though he really cared for me. 'What do you do when you're together, Pat? After all, I take it she's in love with you as well?'

I noticed his mother listening now. I became embarrassed. I loved Noreen a great deal, possibly without showing it. I answered as best I could. 'Well, Lorcan, I simply do as she does. I tend to follow her, kissing, cuddling and that sort— know what I mean?' 'Is that all? Not try anything else?' He stared at me and then quickly glanced towards his mother as though waiting for a signal to go a step further. Suddenly May spoke. 'Look, Pat, you've much to learn, and the sooner you do, the better. There's so much you can do with Noreen that will bind your love. I'll put you in touch with Father Tracy. He's very good at that sort of thing.' I began to wonder what 'thing'? What else is there?

A few days later I sat in front of the priest, an elderly man. I couldn't wait to hear the good news about what Noreen and I were missing out on. I told him my confession. He quickly gave me my penance and shut over the tiny window. I knocked and he reappeared.

'Yes, son, what is it?'

I began to ask him in my own words. 'Well, father, you see … I'm in love with this girl and I believe I should be doing things to make her happy and I've been told to come to you—that you are very good, father, and that you know all about that sort of thing, father.' I waited anxiously for his response.

Suddenly he blurted out, 'Whatever are you talking about, son? Who put you up to this?'

Good God, the sweat oozed out of me in the little dark confessional. 'Someone who knows you, father.'

'Oh, I see—so they couldn't put their finger on it and they want me to do it for you.' He paused. I could hear him sighing, and his breathing was heavy. He spoke quickly now. 'Do you interfere with each other's private parts?'

'Where do you mean, father?' How could I tell him I felt her naked bottom while we kissed in close encounters, as my hands roved beneath her long skirt, but never to the inner side of her. Nor did she touch me in that way. It was a very loving relationship without sex.

'Do you feel each other's bodies?'

'Yes, father.'

'So you've committed mortal sin by your actions.' To cover his embarrassment, which was obvious, he added three decades of the Rosary to my penance, and the Stations of the Cross for good measure. 'Is she Catholic?' he asked.

My heart almost missed a beat. I answered, 'Yes, father,' and waited. He raised his voice. 'The Devil is in both of you, and as he always makes work for idle hands, I suggest both of you join your hands in prayer. I want to see you at the novena and sodality every month.'

I really expected to leave the confessional much wiser than when I first went in, but it was not to be. I came from the church that evening thinking of the night the Apeman had begun to talk to me about the facts of life in Artane. When he learnt I knew nothing about sex or how I came into the world, he began to explain it in a simple way. As he tested my knowledge on life, the more he asked, the less he found I knew about it. So he began to explain about a woman's body. He suddenly put his thumb and forefinger together to produce a circle and said, 'Imagine, boy, that this is a doughnut.' I simply nodded. 'This, then, is the centre passage, and each woman has two.'

I hadn't a clue what he was talking about. Suddenly he decided he had to go as it was very late. Years later, when I left Artane and went to London, I could have done with a fuller explanation.

In 1961, after much deliberation, I knew in my heart and soul I had to go away, as I had no papers or diplomas to prove my skills as a baker. Although I loved Noreen, the desire to do well for myself came first. I will never forget the night I told her. She was never so quiet. If only I had asked her how she felt! I was too full of self-importance, I suppose, always talking about doing the right thing. Though my ideas were good and made sense, I believe I made the wrong decision. It was a shock for her, and it was to change both of our lives. Years later, I knew I had made a bad decision.

I was very much a man with a suitcase during the rest of the 1960s. I travelled to Manchester early in 1961. I kissed Noreen farewell and promised to send for her. As I sat up on the deck of the *Leinster* that night, my mind tossed and turned, and staring at the darkness of the sea all I could think of was my lovely Noreen. But I knew then I had to go on. My heart and mind ached for the one I left behind.

Once in Manchester I found digs, and couldn't wait for

Saturday to go to Old Trafford to see my dream team, Manchester United, who were playing Burnley. After seeing the game I became a United fanatic. But I still had itchy feet, and I didn't like the digs or the city. The house I stayed in was in the district of Chorlton-cum-Hardy, near Medlock. It was a real Irish district. I shared a room with three young men from County Mayo. One of them, called PJ, was sitting in the room with me one day as he wrote a letter to his mother. He looked at me and said, 'It's hard to believe you're a Dublin man. You're so different really, and you haven't got a Dublin Jackeen accent.' I sat there listening, but my mind was elsewhere—perhaps on Noreen.

He tried again. 'You look homesick, Pat. What you need, boy, is a nice girl-friend. 'Twould be the best thing to settle you down.' I simply nodded at him, not knowing how to respond. Then he surprised me. 'You know, Pat, there's nothing better in life, and I mean it now, than spending the night with a lovely sweet girl—I mean sleeping and having intercourse with her; and it's the most wonderful feeling you'll ever get, I promise.'

I sat there agreeing with him, and yet I couldn't really relate to such a young man—only a year or two older than me. I was out of my depth, and I knew it. I thought that night about how experienced he was, and here I was, so gullible and naïve. I began to think then that I was staying with all the wrong people. I knew I had to leave and move on.

After chatting to PJ I learnt about the islands of Guernsey and Jersey. I wasted no time, and booked a flight to Jersey. I was my own worst enemy, running scared, always packing my bags—on my way to somewhere, but it was really never important.

THE flight BEGAN in very bad weather. I was sitting back in my seat, frightened, as the plane took off.

My thoughts were on the girl I left behind me. If only I had been allowed to join the Bakers' Union, I thought, and I cursed myself rather than their system. I should never have become a baker, and I knew that was the whole problem: night work, unsuitable hours, working when everyone else was off—a baker's life is a nightmare, and I knew I would never get a decent position outside of it. Everything I yearned to be, I couldn't be, yet I had a burning desire to be someone. I dreamed of being a writer one day, but judging by my awful attempts at letter writing I reckoned that it would only ever be a dream.

I was all mixed up, and though I wished I could return home, I was most reluctant to. I was desperately in love with Noreen, but I couldn't find it in my heart to relate it in a proper, understanding way to her. I thought my going away would prove a point and I'd feel good about it. In retrospect it was a dreadful mistake to leave the one who meant so much to me.

I was learning everything the hard way, and I had no roots. I was desperately seeking a place to call my own. I was homesick and lovesick, and yet my travels were only beginning.

I glanced around and noticed that the plane was less than half full. Two elderly nuns were praying hard, clutching their Rosary beads, while four English lads were busy playing a game of cards. The rain thundered off the window. I suddenly felt tense and began to pray. After twenty minutes up in the stormy clouds I was sick, along with many other passengers. I really believed I was going to die. I looked again at the nuns and was dismayed to see them on their knees, praying fast and looking as though the end was nigh.

When the plane landed it wasn't Jersey but the seaside town of Bournemouth in England. We were treated to a night in a top-class hotel. I loved it. I decided I liked travel: this was for me! The next day I enjoyed the flight to Jersey.

10

St Brelade's Bay

Jersey in spring I can best describe as a semi-French tropical garden. I quickly fell in love with it. All that filled my teenage mind as I wandered through the narrow cobbled streets of St Helier was, 'I must share this garden of beauty with Noreen.'

I found employment without any real problem as a baker-tablehand in the Sunshine Bakery in St Helier. I worked with a couple of old men; they told me no young people were interested in the trade because of the night work and long, unsociable hours. How right they were! But I was trapped. I remembered the words of Eddie and Matt in the bakery in Fairview, discussing their future over a mug of stewed tea and a smoke. They so often discussed finding a better job. Eddie's last words were always the same: 'Once a bloomin' baker, always a bloomin' baker.' Those words summed up for me the loneliness of the young baker going off to work at a time of night when his mates were going out with girl-friends or for a drink. I was lonely and homesick and working like a slave far from home. But I was over-anxious to get on and make money.

I was going out to work at eleven at night and working harder than I had ever done since I left Artane. I was arriving back in my tiny bedsitter at seven or eight in the morning, feeling like someone who hadn't slept for a week.

The men were getting concerned for me, and knew I didn't look too good. George, the older of the two, suggested I bring over my girl-friend. Old Alf, sitting up on the table and changing his false teeth to eat his supper, spoke very quickly, with a peculiar French accent. 'Every young man needs plenty of it.' Not even realising what it was I needed, I'd simply listen every night to the same talk, listening and thinking of Noreen. Alf would continue: 'You know, Irish, you can't go on masturbating for ever, you know. You'll have to get your girl over here before you go blind.'

I worked with those two old-timers all through the dead of night in 1962, knowing full well how far behind I was in sexual matters. Crudity in the work-place and talk about sex not only confused me but also upset me. I knew I was one of the Brothers' boys: I felt I was better than those I worked with and came into contact with in the bakery trade—which only helped to distance them from me. In reality I was no angel: I was simply short on experience.

I met Noreen at the airport. She hadn't changed a bit. 'What are you thinking?' she asked shyly as I stood back to get a good look at her. 'Well, you, of course. You still look the same—it's as though we were never apart.' She looked amused at me. Her voice was clear as always, with a ring to it. 'You'd think you were away for years, the way you're going on.' She smiled and shook her head, as though she was confused. A bad start, I thought.

I began to dream of more pleasant things as I settled down to life in Jersey with Noreen nearby. No longer was I having nightmares or walking in my sleep. But I started to become anxious, fidgety and cranky in work and out of it. I couldn't even please Noreen in the way she wished. I was always tired, and going to late-night dances at the weekends was out for me.

I never believed for a minute that Noreen would leave me. When she did, I took it as a joke and was overconfident by a mile, assuming that she'd come running back to me. I became very depressed and lonely, but as each day tore at my heart and mind I decided to 'tough it out', as I had been taught to by the Christian Brothers. I loved her, and I believed I had proved beyond doubt my love for her. I never showered her with gifts—that was not my style. When I say 'I love you,' I don't expect gifts in return: just love and respect, and let the rest, whatever it is, follow.

I became a beach stroller along the golden sands of St Quans to the sands of St Brelade's. I often meandered from noon until sunset. I dreaded the loneliness of my tiny bedsitter in the Market Street area of St Helier. I became exhausted from being up all night and beach strolling half the day. I became slimmer, and lovesick rather than homesick.

The summer of 1962 was a scorcher. I hated going out at night to work, and I was blaming the bakery and the long hours for my problems. I decided to go into the market to get a long red rose and a box of chocolates, to make it up and to win back the only one who had ever said, 'I love you.' I walked through the winding streets feeling like a lost child. Finally I came to the guesthouse where Noreen was working and living. I paced up and down for hours on several occasions without ever seeing her.

I now began to realise that Noreen was really gone from me. Whatever love she had had in her young heart seemed to have run cold. My heart wept and ached for the one I loved but whose love for me, for some reason, seemed to evaporate when she arrived in Jersey. I couldn't get to grips with the suddenness of how I lost her, nor the reason why.

I realised there was something strange about the way I related to girls, but the gulf I was desperately trying to bridge only seemed to get wider. Often I was left with the feeling that if only I had tried to be normal and forgotten about my high principles, or if only I tried to distance myself from them and just go out with them without falling in love too soon, it would have been all right. I was far too naïve to please girls, treating them kindly but often with far too much delicacy. If by chance I met any of the girls I adored at their work-place, I often noticed that they were not as polite or as nice as they had acted while out on a date with me, much to my surprise.

As THE SEASON wore steadily on, I was becoming exhausted, having been working up to seventy hours a week, six nights a week. While still hoping for Noreen to come back to me, I took a trip out to St Brelade's Bay one hot Saturday afternoon in August. The weather and the atmosphere were beautiful.

Then I saw Noreen. She was strolling along the hot sands of the bay with a boy-friend, their arms around each other like two beautiful lovers. My heart sank to a new low, and I cried. Then I stepped it out like a soldier, and went for a walk along the country roads.

As I made my way along a narrow country lane, I was sure I had heard a cry for help. I looked about, waited, then a second cry. There was a low hedge, and I hurried towards it, past what looked like a mansion—a big farmhouse, I guessed at a glance. I noticed a scooter lying over the ditch, and below it a young woman in some distress. My lucky day! I smiled at the thought.

My depressed feeling vanished as I said, 'I'd be glad to be of some help to you.' 'Thank you. Help me out of here.' She smiled up at me and added, 'I've got punctured tyre and hurt shoulder. Please can you fix puncture for me?' I was thrilled to be of some help. When she spoke again I fell in love with her French accent, and the way she smiled helped to erase any thoughts of Noreen. 'I'm Maria Duvarre. Please help me with scooter. I live next to farmhouse, where I work as au pair. The family are away.' I introduced myself, and fell over the scooter. 'Damn it,' I said. With a neat flick of her hand she brushed back her long auburn hair and laughed loudly as I lay across it. 'Oh, you Irish, you are funny people.' I hadn't told her I was Irish.

Having repaired the puncture for her, I was dripping with sweat. As I stood gazing about, wondering where I could wash myself, I suddenly heard her voice calling. 'Patrick, Patrick, please come and you have shower. You are so dirty and hot.' I looked about to see where she was, and there she was up on the balcony of the big stone farmhouse, dressed in a bathrobe. My heart missed a beat. No more 'if onlys,' I hoped.

My mind suddenly began to focus on my lost love, and I began to see the face of Noreen as I entered the huge house. Once inside I was instantly attracted by the magnificent staircase. Maria appeared. I became flushed as she stood in her pink bathrobe, gesturing to me to come up. 'I'm the maid. The family are visiting some people in St Peter Port.' 'Where's that?' 'It is in Guernsey,' she said. 'Now you need shower, Patrick—perhaps then we have drink. You Irish love your drink.' She smiled at me, but little did she realise that I never drank alcohol.

She seemed a few years older than me. I was determined to go along with Maria to please her but also, more impor-tant to me, for the experience. It's now or never, I thought! The moment I got a whiff of her perfume I was in a state of complete paralysis beneath the shower, as her body touched mine. Suddenly I had the most wonderful feeling I had ever experienced. I lost all control as I entered the world of love. We passionately caressed each other while the cool water flowed down on us.

She held the glasses of sparkling champagne and placed the bottle on the floor. She held a glass up to me and as I took hold of it, we touched glasses. A beautiful feeling came over me. As I was always a fast drinker—of tea or minerals, that is—no sooner had I downed my first than she filled it again. For the first time I realised I was intoxicated. 'My God, what have I done! I've broken my pledge!' I felt awful at that thought, really hurt. I closed my eyes for a silent moment, my pride hurt beyond repair. 'I'll have a lot to con-fess next time,' I muttered. Maria looked at me with a smile. 'You speak, Patrick? Tell me, I like you very much, so you make me very happy.' I must be doing something right, as

Maria was so happy and contented. I couldn't get myself to express fully how wonderful I felt.

Knowing I was not properly able to cope with the situation I found myself in, I was ever conscious of the fact that I could fail. Maria's voice was a low, tempting whisper. 'What are you thinking of, Irish?' She smiled. I feared the thoughts of having to leave her, though I knew in my heart I would have to go. In so many ways this was like another golden day out in a wonderful dream, filled with passion. But as Maria spoke again, I realised it was true, and I loved it.

'You need towel, Irish. It's here. Come, you'll see. Hope you don't mind me call you Irish, Patrick.' I opened my eyes and suddenly felt, I can do this, damn it. I'll go as far as she is prepared to go.

Maria was waiting in the open door with a long bath towel. I could taste the breathtaking sweetness of her fragrance as she began to towel me. What am I to do? Just let it happen, I told myself. I must do this my way. Then the thought struck me. What way is that? I smiled. It's got to be her way or I'm a goner, I thought.

As she led me onto her, she slowly fell backwards onto the huge old bed with velvet canopy. For a while I felt I was lying beneath a chapel dome, though in reality I was on top of beautiful Maria. Suddenly I knew I had to try it.

There was total silence. I was hoping Maria would lead the way; the last thing I wanted now was for me to mess it all up and be left feeling sorry for myself.

Briefly I thought of Noreen, and how I lost her. Then I felt Maria's fingers dig deep into my flesh, her mouth open wide on mine. Her fingers tore into my flesh. What do I do now? I wanted her to do something about the way I felt. I was burning up, ready to scream. 'It's not in, Irish. It's not in yet.' I wanted her to help me, not so that I could blame her but in reality because I didn't know how. If only the Apeman had continued his attempt at sex education that night in the dormitory instead of leaving it unfinished.

Then Maria gently took hold of me, and I experienced the

ecstasy of love. As the essence of love flowed I went wild with passion. Maria cried out with joy for the fulfilment it gave her. Suddenly I cried, 'I've done it!' I felt so proud! As I lay on my back I felt sorry as the dreadful thought struck me: I'd committed a mortal sin—but at least I was normal. I'll confess later, I thought, glancing at Maria's nakedness. I simply adored looking. Her body left me spellbound.

Maria reached for the wine glasses. She smiled as she handed me the full glass and said, 'You make me so happy. It was so good. I'd love to have you to stay whole night but I'm not allowed to have friends after eleven o'clock at night. See, I must go by the rules of this house, okay, Patrick?' I wanted to remain in this fragrant garden for as long as my heart beat. I could feel her lips touching my shoulders and slowly finding their way to my lower back. I rolled over. I could see the hunger in her brown eyes. I wept with joy as we both cried out in ecstasy.

After a long moment she spoke. 'Tell me, Irish, what you thinking of?' She filled out more wine. 'Now, Irish, take this. Does you so much good, I see. Makes you act with more passion.' I was scared of ending this sea of love, though I suddenly realised my passion for more had subsided. She spoke, playing her lips on mine. 'What's in your mind now, Irish, you so quiet?' I couldn't tell her that my head was soaring, that I was a teetotaller. She'd laugh at me for certain.

She closed in against me. Her lips began a passionate sensual trail along the flat of my stomach. I could see that she was more than anxious to be pleased again. I knew there was no way so soon. Then the awful thought struck me as I raised my head. The room was going round again. 'I'm drunk. I've lost my pledge. Oh, God!' I said out loud. I never expected I had to please Maria so much.

Maria was on top of me. Her voice was soft. 'You look sad, Irish.' She stroked her fingers along my thighs and rested there. My eyes began to feel heavy. I wanted to sleep beneath Maria's beautiful body. As her lips played on mine, 'tis Heaven without saints, I thought, and suddenly laughed.

The room grew darker. I must have dozed off. Maria's hands reached around my head and she swiftly pulled me onto her. All the fire of my love released itself in a burst of passion as her lips met mine in a heavenly embrace. I gazed into her eyes appealingly, silently pleading with her to understand my inability to please her again. There was no abating her hunger. I really had to try, though, but how it hurt! I felt awful, and my expression hardened. Her eyes swiftly met mine. I was relieved. 'Is that it, Irish?' She smiled up at me encouragingly, and her voice healed my bruised ego. 'I will never forget you, Irish.' She paused for a brief moment, smiled, and said, 'Au revoir Patrick, thank you for fixing my tyre.'

11

A Picture of You

In October I was back home in Fairview, working for James Behan in the bakery in Fairview Strand, and once again I was welcomed by May and Lorcan Mooney in Cadogan Road.

While I was playing soccer in Fairview Park one Saturday with a few ex-Artane lads and a team from Fairview, there was a schools hurling match on the pitch beside us. I had noticed the Drisco, who I worked under as a cook and a kitchener in Artane, and also a few other Christian Brothers; but the one who got most of my attention was the Macker. That Brother looked every bit as tall and as hard as the time he battered my best pal, Minnie Kelly, around the head and face with his open hands until he told him where he had hidden a pencil in the dormitory. Poor Minnie gave in. The silly pencil was found in a flower pot on the window ledge, and the next morning poor Minnie was practically unrecognisable.

I was close to the Macker as he stood on the sideline watching the team when suddenly I heard him call me, using my Artane nickname. 'Collie.' I walked up to him. 'You called me, sir?' I stood looking up at the man who so often beat me with his dreadful leather for such silly things as being caught out of bed swapping a *Dandy* or a *Beano* with a lad a few beds away. I had slept with fear of that tall Christian Brother whenever he was in charge of our dormitory: fear of wetting my bed and of being flogged by him for it. His voice was soft, and I felt sadness for the man who was once my master, who had shown me and my pals no mercy or any kind of love. He slowly reached his right hand into an inside pocket and pulled out a wallet. He spoke quickly and smiled as he did so. 'I've got something to show you, Collie. Do they still call you that?' 'No, sir, not now. They call me Paddy or Pat now.'

I watched him open out the wallet and take out an envelope. 'I've got a picture of you, Pat, and a few of your pals from Barnacullia.' He handed them to me. 'But it's me, sir, making my Confirmation, and one of my pals too. How did you keep them so good, sir, for so long?' I looked again at them. I noticed all the lads who were in my class that year, back in 1954. He suddenly handed me the envelope and said, 'Keep them, Collie. I've had them long enough now. I suspect you're keeping well and out of trouble, as so many have problems, you know. Keep up your prayers and go to Mass.' He turned and walked away.

I met that Brother several times after that, riding his bike through Fairview, and he always stopped and chatted to me, always giving me sound advice. After each occasion we met I understood more of the man and the fact that the shadow of Artane had left its mark on him also.

It struck me then that it is never too late to change. I also understood his reasons for wishing me to go my own way and to keep my distance from other Artaners. I'm sure he never meant any harm by that, as I learnt much more when I mixed with lads who were lucky to have had a decent childhood. I was a slow learner in Artane, and I believe the system and fear of the Brothers kept me back a great deal.

Often I was told by my old boss Mick Bradley that I carried a chip on my shoulder and that I was overpowering, too talkative and too loud for people to take to me. I met Mick as I left the park that evening and as usual he ended the conversation by giving me sound advice, pointing out that I marched everywhere. In fact I very much wanted to be noticed.

ONE MORNING I arrived for work at four in Behan's bakery. I was met by Eddie, and I could see that something was bothering him. A hangover, I supposed, and breezed by him in the hall. The bakery, although an extension, was part of the house. The oddest thing was that it faced out onto the back of Mick Bradley's Pure Buttermilk Home Bakery. Matt was now the foreman and Mando was his second in command, and young Sweetman, an ex-Artane lad I knew well, worked there also.

When I looked across the back yard that morning I was slow to notice that the lights of Bradley's were out. As I came from the changing room I looked towards Eddie. He looked pale and was silent. Then I became aware of the quietness of the place. It's unreal, I thought; it's not like the lads in there to be so quiet.

Eddie pulled out the stool and, like an old man, rested himself, warily lit up a Woodbine, and drew heavily on it. I was fresh and all eager to get going, as was my usual way. As I began to prepare for work Eddie said, 'There's no need, Paddy, for that, not this morning. Poor Mick Bradley is gone.' I was numb, and I shook all over. 'Dead?' I asked stupidly. He grew angry and snapped, 'Yes, dead. You know what it means. Snuffed it, Paddy! For Christ's sake go home.'

As I stood in the biting early winter east wind in the small old Sutton Cemetery, my thoughts were not on the prayers for the dead but rather on the time the big Derry man marched boldly across the wooden floor of my dormitory in the Catholic Boys' Home to see me. I thought of all the good things Mick Bradley had done for me and for Mando and the lads ... my first trip ever on an aeroplane. 'Oh, Lord, why take such a dear man away?'

While the prayers for the dead were being said, I cast my eye around the mourners—mostly tall, elderly men. The east wind seemed to cut straight through me. Suddenly I noticed a gap at the graveside and the coffin being lowered. The priest was reading out the sequence. I felt the ground trembling beneath my feet as I stood on soft, loose clay. I gazed down and I wept for a gentle, kind Derry man—'salt of the earth,' I thought as I listened to the sequence. I dropped a single rose to rest below.

Judge of justice, please hear my prayer,
Spare me, dear Lord, in mercy spare,
Now the reckoning day appear.
Worthless are my prayers, I know,
Yet oh, cause me not to go into everlasting woe.

I had been sent to him as a young lad, to serve him. I hope I did well for him, and what work I did I knew I did it with a good heart. I loved the big, tall Derry man. May he rest in peace.

AT THE TURN of 1963 things were not really working out in the Home Bakery. I found working with some of the lads a bit too much. The wages were awfully low: four pounds ten shillings. I told Jim I would have to leave if he couldn't give me a rise of at least ten bob—50p. In response he drew out a right, and I hit the floor. After a punch-up we ended up shaking hands in Clontarf Garda station; and I did get a small increase after that.

From 1960 to 1968 I seemed to be working between Ireland, England, and Jersey. I got that bug about working in Jersey for the summer season. Each time I'd return to Dublin I would stay with one of my old landladies. I went back to Mooneys in Fairview quite a lot.

No matter how I tried to better myself, I had no real qualifications for anything: not even bakery work, let alone anything more satisfying. Desperate to make a break out of the trade, I wrote to the ESB for work. When word came to report for work in Milltown, opposite Shamrock Rovers' grounds, I got my bakery gear and threw it in the dustbin. I won't forget boasting to the lads in the bakery that I was finished for all time with night work and unsociable hours. I felt great that at last I had done it!

The foreman stood alongside a truck. The back of it was open, and I could see the picks and shovels. I was shocked. I put my hand into my pocket to get the letter regarding the position that I believed was to change my life. I read it carefully. It simply stated that I was to report for work at the site outside the football club and to meet the site foreman at half eight. I had assumed it was for an indoor position and general work.

By half eight there were about forty lads, each waiting for their new start. The site foreman sent me to break up the road with a pick, along with twenty others. As we worked, the next team were to dig the trench for the pipe-laying, as far as Ringsend. The foreman was a huge man. When I spoke to him he sounded pig-ignorant as he grunted back at me, 'Get digging, and keep digging. We stop at half ten for fifteen minutes—now dig, boy.' I was shocked, as were the others. Many simply threw their pick or shovel down and left, and by half ten, out of over forty who started, twenty remained.

By one o'clock I was dead beat, my smooth hands blistered, bruised, cut, and bleeding. I walked away to get the bus into the city. In Fleet Street I drew on my Artane courage and marched boldly through the offices of the ESB until I found the manager's office. I was furious and felt like turning the table over on him. He looked at me in amazement. 'Yes, son, what's your problem?' I read him the riot act and explained my predicament and the dreadful way I was being mistreated. When I showed him how the letter never explained what the position was in Milltown, he was amazed. But I was now out of a job. So much for change!

WHILE WAITING AT Dublin Airport for my flight to Jersey, I came face to face with my former drill master, better known as Driller the Killer. With him was none other than the famous Brother nicknamed the Hellfire, dressed in casual clothes. As I sat down and waited for my flight number to be called, I thought of those two Christian men.

Hellfire, who taught me for two years, got his nickname from producing pictures of Hell and scaring the children in the classroom with them. He beat boys' naked buttocks so badly that the blood seeped through their shorts. He often made me stand out facing the wall with my hands held above my head for long periods; if I let my hands drop, he would beat the legs off me. Driller the Killer was no ordinary drill instructor. He beat lads so badly that they were often removed to hospital or to the infirmary. Some lads never returned.

ONCE BACK IN St Helier my old boss, Graham, quickly offered me my job back and asked me to stay for the coming season. I took up the sport I had been banned from playing in Artane: I joined a soccer club, and enjoyed the forbidden game.

The Channel Islands in the 1960s were a great source of comfort and therapy for me, though I always had a longing to return to Ireland. Hearing Irish songs and music always made me feel emotional, especially while working through the night.

When I'd meet a girl who was pleased to go out with me, I'd fall in love with her instantly. My naïveté and gullibility only showed up more my utter immaturity. But the loves that I lost in those enchanting islands were to change me and my whole attitude in later years.

In Jersey in 1967 I fell overboard in love with a school-teacher from Yorkshire. I wrote to Carmella O'Grady, informing her that I expected to be sending her and Carine an invitation to come to Jersey to my wedding! I was so excited and in love that I was working all night and on the beach most of the day. I was really in love with a girl whom I would have walked on water to have and to hold.

Helen was from Bingley in Yorkshire. She taught in a national school in St Helier. She was mature, tall, nicely attractive without being beautiful. Her green eyes and short fair hair matched her beautiful warm smile and complexion. She spoke very clearly, and I fell for her sweet voice the moment she agreed to dance an old-time waltz with me. I still recall the tune, which was a hit at the time from the Mario Lanza film *The Student Prince*. She called me Larry: it was my middle name, and she preferred it to Paddy in front of her English friends. I was floating rather than walking—or was I walking into it again?

I received a letter from Carmella that brought me down to earth for a while, but I took no heed whatsoever of its sound advice, and rushed foolishly onwards.

Helen was a superb swimmer, and the weather in April that year was simply lovely. I couldn't swim and I had a fear of water since my school days in Artane. Helen stood on the wide sea wall; the tide was full in. The sea was calm and very tempting. She dived in and shouted for me to follow. I looked into the deep blue water. It was a good forty yards to the far side of the walled-in section where we were.

Although I couldn't swim, I felt confident I'd get help if I got into difficulties. I was studying every stroke Helen was making. When she shouted again for me to come in, I dived in; my belly hit the water with some force and felt it. I fought with all my strength to stay on top. My arms were frantically cutting like propellers. My right hand began the pattern: straight out, hand cutting into the water and pulling it back, only to send my left hand out to repeat the move, as I had watched Helen do.

I was shocked when she suddenly dived on top of me, pulling me beneath the water. My shorts loosened, and as I struggled to come up I lost them down around my ankles. I scrambled to the safety of the sea wall, and with difficulty I climbed up. I was dreadfully embarrassed, though relieved by the look on Helen's face as she climbed up. She broke out in a long, loud burst of laughter. Her big beach towel came in most useful.

The first time I went to her flat was to collect her to go to a meeting where she was to lecture. When I got there I noticed that she was neither getting ready nor acting as though she was preparing to go out. She was in fact sitting on the floor, her back resting against her divan bed. There was a sign over her bed with a big letter L in red, standing out like a beacon. I smiled then as I thought of Maria.

Slowly I moved closer to Helen. God, how I wanted her! The more she corrected the homework the more I loved watching her, as she had a true love for the children and her work. As I sat beside her I felt that in many ways she would make up for my lost loves. In some ways I looked upon her as a mother; my mind was at sea with the love I had to offer.

Suddenly I remembered to invite her to a special old-time dance in the Intercontinental Hotel. She agreed.

We shared a bottle of French wine as we enjoyed a salad supper. She became happy and boisterous and began to chase me around the flat. Suddenly she began to act as a teacher. She was letting herself go—a way of relaxing or letting out all the tension in her, I supposed. I was amazed at her wild acts and sense of fun.

While I waited for her to answer the phone, I sat on her low single bed, ever conscious of the L sign above it. When she reappeared I was shocked. She came towards me carrying a ruler, dressed only in her bra and pink frilly panties. She was ever so strong for a woman, I thought, as she began to wrestle with me to get them off and began slapping my bottom. 'You're a naughty boy, Larry,' she shouted. 'I slap naughty boys for not doing their homework.' As I broke free from her, I landed on the floor.

Her lips seemed to play on mine for a long time. Her breasts were full and round; my lips made a heavenly trail through the velvet parting. 'Oh, Larry, you shouldn't. You're not really like that. I can tell you're trying so hard to please. I do love you; but Gloria and I have made plans to go to Australia. If only we met six months ago! Oh, Larry, you mustn't.' But my hunger for love and the French wine had overpowered me. There's no way back from this, I thought.

Helen pressed her body on top of mine. Suddenly we rolled over and over. She began to play her naughty games. I couldn't resist. I managed to get hold of her smacking hand. 'My bottom has had enough,' I said. She giggled; I was glad when she stopped. The silence in the room was tempting. I felt the warmth of her moist lips on mine. I cried, 'My God, I love you. Stay with me.' It was hopeless. Her plans were made. Yet it had no effect on how I felt for her. I wanted to remain in the warmth of her embrace for as long as Heaven allowed. When she spoke again I realised I'd have to go. Our lips met. 'I'll see you at the hotel, Larry. We shall be true friends, I promise you.'

I couldn't wait for the night of the old-time dance the following Saturday. I had no fears about missing work, as it was my only night off.

The dance floor was bigger than I expected. Helen danced like a professional. 'You're full of surprises,' I said, as we waited for the next waltz to be played. The tables were lit by candlelight, which added to the warmth and romance that filled the ballroom. The music was slow now, a sensual waltz. I couldn't keep my eyes off Helen, as I realised that it could well be our last dance. I was heartbroken.

I could feel her hands low, below my waist. I felt so starved of being loved I was ready to tear her clothes off. She didn't resist my lips as they smothered her mouth. My hand tightly around her bottom, I could feel her press hard into me.

As the music stopped we were in a dark corner alone. 'Larry, please take me,' she pleaded. After a moment she changed her mind and cried, 'Stop, hold it.' For me it was too late. 'Poor Larry, where to now?' I dreaded the thought.

I couldn't get Helen out of my lovesick mind. She warned me not to get too close to her, as she had plans made with her best friend in Bolton. I became heartbroken in my struggle to hold on to a love I had won. But I'd have to swallow my defeat and soldier on. I was again so close to the love of my dreams, only to see those dreams fade and die.

Towards June of that year, Helen's friend from Bolton joined her and shared the flat with her. Helen and I walked for miles along the golden sand of St Quans as she poured out her thoughts to me. 'I have so much to tell you, Larry, and I have to apologise for a few things.' I was amazed at her words. 'I fell in love with you. I had promised myself and Gloria that I wouldn't get involved with men or have an affair, as Gloria and I are leaving for Sydney in September or October—so you see, Larry, it's not your fault at all that we can't be in love and together. I love you as a friend, but I have to draw the line. If we don't go in the autumn we will definitely be going by Easter. You're welcome to come to Bingley and stay for a few days before I go.'

God, how I cried as she held me close in her arms! I clung to her, falling and rolling on the sand. We stayed that way for a long while. Our lips met in a passionate kiss and our arms embraced.

'Perhaps you'll write a poem before I go?' I promised her I would. I knew then it was over. At least she was leaving me on friendly terms and not because I was no good.

As she left, I was surprised when she stopped and turned. I stood up and began to hurry towards her. 'You can come and stay for a few days before I leave. Okay, Larry?' I was thrilled. I couldn't wait for the day when I'd meet her again.

IT WAS THE end of July. Life must go on, I told myself, and I tried hard to pick up the pieces. I disappointed Graham in the Sunshine Bakery when I told him I was getting out of the bakery trade. The night work and constant loss of sleep, combined with bad and irregular eating habits, were destroying me. Though he was annoyed, he agreed with me. Sadly, it was the last occasion I was to see him, as he died after a severe illness.

When I went to leave that evening, the manager of the shop called me. 'An English lady left this for you.' I took hold of the bag and walked out, wondering what was inside it. Once away from the shop, I was pleased to see the photographs she had left for me. I still have many of them today.

THE CHANCE OF a change of job came about, and quite a change it was too: in the Sunshine Knitwear Factory in St

Helier. I got word that I was to start at a quarter past nine on the Monday morning. I didn't know myself, going out to work at that hour. The lunch hour was from half twelve to half one, and as the weather was extremely hot, the staff went down the road to West End Park.

I was just into my second week, and all was going well. The heat inside the factory was stifling, and I couldn't wait to get out for the break and go sunbathing in the park. At last I've made the right decision, I thought.

As I hurried along, my mind was on the loves I had won and lost. Suddenly Noreen entered my mind. I thought of the times I had sat by the rose bed with her and passionately kissed and caressed her. I kissed her lips a thousand times since in my dreams. My heart had been filled with woe when Noreen went away, and now I had to suffer again.

When I arrived at West End, the park was at its colourful best. I lay down under the hot sun, and when I woke up my face and back were soaked with sweat. I looked at my watch. 'Gosh, it's twenty-five past one! I'll be late.' I went to run, but felt rather odd; and as the days passed I knew there was something very wrong indeed.

12

Near Death Do I Sleep

At the Saturday night dance at the Intercontinental Hotel, I fell into the arms of a Liverpool lass. At nineteen, Susan was more mature than many much older women. I began by asking her for her name, when suddenly I fell against her. The room seemed to be going round, and I could feel her hands touching me and asking, 'Are you drunk, Patrick?' It was then she realised I didn't drink. She decided to bring me outside into the warm night air and then back to her hotel.

I might not be here at all but for Susan and my roommate Bill. 'You really do look odd,' Susan said. 'Blimey, Irish, where does it hurt?' I muttered, 'Oh, God, how my head aches!' She lay me down on her bed, whispering softly, 'I'll cure you, I promise, Irish.' She lay down on top of me; but my mind was far from what she wanted. She simply couldn't understand how sick I was. My body ached from the light; my head was dizzy.

She tried everything to arouse me. She went round the room half naked. I couldn't respond. 'I picked a right one tonight then, mate!' I was in a trance, while Susan was doing her best to tempt me. Finally she said, 'Gosh, Irish, you must be bloody well sick, 'cause if you're not, then you're bloomin' queer! You need a doctor.'

I heard her all right, but I didn't realise where she was. I forced myself up off the bed, and, amazingly, I could stand up. I could walk, but found that my breathing was strange. As I moved about I suddenly fell on top of Susan's naked body. She went wild! I must have passed out. When I recovered, she was towelling my forehead. I was glad to see she had put her clothes back on.

Her final words as I left were, 'Go to a doctor, Irish, or it's an early resting place. I wanted you more than I wanted any lad, Irish.' I scrambled to my bedsitter, which I shared with two English lads and Billy from Dundee. That night I slept close to death. I couldn't breathe, hardly able to ask for help. The next day Bill took me to the hospital.

The Scottish doctor was a huge, heavily built man. I didn't like him. 'What's your problem, fella? You look the fittest man here.' 'I've got an odd feeling, with a sore, heavy head and lightness at times.' He moved slowly towards me, possibly fearful that he would catch whatever I had. He shouted at me, 'Open up your mouth.' Then he decided what was wrong with me. 'A wee touch of flu, lad. You shouldn't ever come in here with that. Get out and don't come back. You Irish are all the same—a mere cough and you're worried sick! Off with you, lad!'

GRAVE DE LEC was a beautiful quaint place for a day by the sea. For me it had that special French touch. The young holidaymakers came in their droves to lie on the sand. It was so colourful—heaven on earth, but hell to me. I thought I was going to die. It was stifling hot, and I was tempted to dive into the water, as I knew how to swim now, thanks to Helen. But something told me not to go near the water.

Bill, my flatmate from Dundee, advised me to go and see a doctor again. I laughed at him, after what had happened at the hospital. 'Right, then, go to a chemist's shop and explain to them how you feel. You look like death, and if you go in for a swim, I've no money to bury you.'

I walked into the chemist's shop, only a few doors from the Sunshine Bakery, and I thought of Graham and how he died. A young assistant came towards me. 'Are you all right?'

'I need something for a headache, if you don't mind.' I moved towards a chair. I noticed her talking to a man in a white coat, though I couldn't hear them. She came quickly over to me, and put a glass of water and two tablets down on the glass shelf. 'Now, if you don't mind, I've been advised to take your temperature. It's nothing for you to worry about, now. It's just that we like to take precautions.'

I thought nothing of it, and let her get on with it. I gazed about the shop. I did notice the staff watching me. I wished I could be like them: working in a chemist's shop, dressed so neatly, with decent working hours. The assistant taking my temperature looked at me in surprise, then hurried away. Within moments I was led to a room upstairs; there the doctor came to examine me. I still thought nothing of it, until the doctor asked me if I had any problem about going into hospital. I said I had none but that I had been thrown out of the hospital just over a week earlier. He was shocked. 'Well, son, they won't throw you out again, and I mean it. It's a matter of urgency that you get in at once. Your temperature is 105 degrees and rising. I'll call for help.'

He told me I had a severe form of meningitis, and that the doctor who had sent me away from the hospital had a lot to answer for. 'The ambulance is on its way.' At that moment I longed to be home—home in Ireland, to whichever landlady would care to put me up. 'God, don't let me die here,' I silently prayed.

My mind was going round in circles. I wished I was back in Dublin. I cried for Helen, who had only recently said goodbye to me, though she was still on the island. I cried for her love to touch me; I longed for her and yearned to see the smile on her face, to touch once more her velvet lips.

I went through agony on that first night in hospital. Seven or eight doctors and nurses struggled with me while one of them extracted fluid from my back, naked and bent over on my knees. I was never so embarrassed or so sick. After they got what they needed I was put lying flat in a darkened room. My head really ached. I was inspected every few hours; my bottom was being punctured like a tyre going over a bed of nails for several weeks.

I was shocked to see the big Scottish doctor enter my room, with his team of interns. 'Oh, God, not him,' I groaned. He spoke a good deal more politely, and he sounded apologetic too. 'How are you now, Patrick?' I tried to lift up my head, but it hurt too much.

For a month I lay on the flat of my back. If only someone could tell Noreen I was here, or even Helen, who was not a mile away from the hospital—but I realised it was wishful thinking. No visitors were allowed. My heart pined for Helen, like a child in desperate need of its mother.

The big doctor realised he had made a bad error, and each morning he came to see me it showed. He made amends, with the aid of a terrific staff, which was a relief to him and a gift of life to me.

THE LONELINESS I felt when I left the hospital was too much for me. I broke down, and was brought back to the hospital. The staff could not have been more helpful. They found a lodging house for me, and as the days wore on I built up my strength. I walked the golden sands, from West Park to the end of St Quans. I met Helen's flatmate from Bolton, and we walked for miles. I was glad to learn they were not leaving for Australia until the following April. I promised her I'd take up Helen's offer to visit her in Bingley, and that I'd have her poem for her.

As I gained strength, I was most reluctant to lie down on the beach or lie in the sun, for fear I'd fall asleep. I remembered the last words of the big Scottish doctor: 'Mad dogs and Englishmen go out in the mid-day sun.'

BY SEPTEMBER I was fit and well. I wanted to return to Ireland, but I knew I had to have a holiday. Scotland was the place to see, and I could get the train to Yorkshire to see Helen before it was too late. I intended to stay in Aberdeen for a few weeks, then move on to Bradford, which was the nearest city to Bingley.

Once in Aberdeen I almost got hitched in the first week. I fell in love with Aberdeen, and it helped me to find myself. The dreadful depression that had crept over me after leaving the hospital began to fade. Within a few days in the city I was working in the biggest bakery, on the night shift. But I was not able for the hard graft. I knew I would have to pack in the job.

The Saturday night dance in the Modern Ballroom was the place to be. I dressed neatly, as I was trained to do by the Brothers. I felt at home in Aberdeen. It was so much like Dublin, I thought.

I wasted no time in asking a lassie up to dance. To my surprise I found the task much more simple than I had expected. The ballroom was crowded by midnight. A 'ladies' choice' was called, and the MC advised the men that it was a rule of the house that they couldn't refuse. After all, it's only a dance, I thought; but at the back of my mind was the thought that I could well be dancing with my future wife.

I was asked up to dance. I waltzed with a very attractive young woman from Glasgow. She seemed rather shy and distant, but she was a lovely dancer, and I admired her so much that I wanted to return the compliment when they next called an old-time waltz.

When we danced again it was to the music of 'The Northern Lights of Old Aberdeen'. The crowd actually began singing while they waltzed. This time round, my partner was more forthcoming and I got her name.

Nora was of slim build. Her dark shoulder-length hair and hazel eyes gave her a very romantic appearance though she had a faraway look about her, and as far as romance was concerned, it was in no way an integral part of her make-up. She agreed to let me walk her home to her flat. We stood in the dark hallway. I reached to kiss her, with my hands resting on her shoulders, and was shocked when she swiftly smacked me hard across the face. 'Good God, what did you do that for?' Then another smack! I tried to get out of the dark hall and shouted, 'Where's the light? I've got to go.' I kept my distance. Then Nora invited me up for tea!

Though pretty Nora was attractive, I found her somewhat cold on romance. I liked warm-hearted girls, rather than those who blew hot and cold or acted as though they were some kind of tap that you turned on or off. After two weeks going together, Nora brought me up to somewhere in the Highlands to meet her parents. Her friends gathered round. Soon I was to realise what was coming next. As I spoke to one of her five sisters I was amazed to hear that Nora's family were expecting an early wedding!

After the third week Nora really astonished me when she got a bedsitter in the same house where I was lodging. Though it went well enough, I found she was all over me— so much so that I couldn't go out without her permission. Yet I liked her, though she was no Maria, nor had she the charisma of Helen.

I was driven off to meet her family one evening, and I took care to notice many things. I learnt plenty about Nora. I realised that she was most anxious to get married, and that I would be suitable. I was a non-drinker and non-smoker, while she smoked like an old chimney and drank her Scotch the way I drank tea. The thought of getting a few smacks while she was sober was one thing, and that was only for trying to kiss her ... well, it scared me to think what she might do if she had a few drams of Scotch too many. I knew I had to get to hell out as fast as I could. But where on earth could I go? Without much real thought, I decided to get the train to Bradford and to visit Helen in Bingley. As I recalled her saying, 'It's Yorkshire for me.'

13

Bradford Royal

I sat alone in the comfortable carriage for the journey south, and as the train pulled out I thought of Helen and thanked God. I believe in God, who gives me hope.

When the train crossed the border my mind was filled with pleasant thoughts of Helen as I had known her in Jersey. I tried to visualise what her home in Bingley was like.

In many ways I was wrong to be getting so close to an old flame, even though it was only for a few days. I realised I could never hope to win her heart, as she was booked to go to Australia. But the call of the flesh was too much for me to fight off. I would not keep my distance once I set eyes on her. I was about to land on my face.

Thoughts of sunny Jersey came flooding to my mind on that bus ride to Bingley, which was only about six miles from Bradford. I was still in love with Helen, and thought of the time she spanked my bottom. I loved the idea of someone I loved so much doing that. I wondered why she had to cross the world to prove she was a good teacher. What I'd give to keep her ... but once again I was gripped by my feeling of inferiority, and I finally realised that it was the girls I loved to love that I could never have, which made me lust after them with such hunger.

The bus pulled up in the village just before the bridge. When I got off I could see Helen waiting, as she had promised in her letter. Below the bridge the Aire River flowed gently by. I put my case down and smiled as I looked at Helen. Her short hair was more blonde, I thought. Her eyes sparkled like the clear water of the river below. As we embraced, I could hear car horns and whistles, even shouts. We both wondered what on earth it was for. Then I noticed Helen's short, tight mini-skirt, showing a fine naked thigh.

For a few days I stayed in the lovely village, which reminded me so much of old-fashioned Christmas cards. I walked with Helen for miles along the green banks of the Aire and gazed at the old mills close to the water's edge. She told me, 'If I had to remain in England for ever, I'd like you to know that I'd want to share it with you, Larry—but I've got a teaching position in Australia, and I've got to go. But I know I've hurt you. You know, I heard about your stay in hospital from Gloria in Bolton. I was shocked to hear how near you'd been to the end—how I could have helped you through it, Larry.'

Without thinking, I pleaded, 'Please don't go. You don't have to. Bingley is so peaceful.' I reached out. She was in my arms. Our lips met in a passionate and loving embrace.

How I longed to possess her by the banks of the Aire. We lay down by an old oak tree. 'Whatever will you do, Larry? You can't stay here, not without me.' Suddenly I said, 'I'll look for the nearest bakery and get work.' She laughed. 'Oh, Larry, not in Bingley! It's far too small a place. It's worse than Jersey. You're kidding.' Then she really amazed me. 'Come to Australia with us.' The thought of all that sun, the heat! How could I get through that sort of climate? My heart beat faster, until finally I responded, and how it hurt me to say, 'I'm so sorry.' I believe she knew I'd say no.

We lay down, my head resting against the tree. 'Why not try New Zealand, Larry? And perhaps if you like it there you might come and see us in Sydney.' I agreed. I'd go to New Zealand, and drop over to see her in Sydney.

I couldn't wait to book my passage on the first available ship to New Zealand. It was for the end of November. I paid over my savings of £170, which left me broke.

As the time slowly passed, I was on a perpetual high as I went to work in Emilio's Bakery in Bradford. I felt as though I was in a wonderful, everlasting dream. On Sundays I would head for Shipley Glen and wander through the thick growth, pushing or stamping on the bracken and thorn to find my way to the green mossy slopes of the Aire River.

I wrote my poem for Helen, and called it 'It's Yorkshire for Me'. I read it to her when we met for the last time by the Aire. When I had finished, she turned to me and said, 'Oh, Larry, you're such a romantic!' She smiled, wiped her eyes, and in a swift movement her arms were embracing me. Her moist lips covered mine in a passionate movement. The heat of her body was overpowering for me; as I lay on top of her, I could hear her heartbeat. 'I know you're in love with me,' she said, then she drew a breath and added, 'You promised me you wouldn't.' She didn't feel my gentle fingers open her blouse, as my lips, hungry with passion, found joy close to the heart that I longed to win. She whispered, 'Oh, Larry, you shouldn't. I love you. I love you. You promised me you wouldn't.'

ALONE AGAIN IN my new lodgings, I felt a terrific loss. I sat and pondered for hours on end. I had to look to the future.

Whenever I looked at my ticket for the liner, I could feel the tension mixed with a strange sort of excitement. Suddenly it began to frighten me—going so very far away. I received a letter from Dr Alan O'Grady. He promised me he would always be a guardian to me. Soon I received a first bon voyage card, signed *Gloria*. (I still have it.) Suddenly I felt I had lost anyone who ever got close to loving me.

I kept up the hard work I was doing in Emilio's. I was working in the pastry plant with a local chap called Simon. We were making thousands of sausage rolls and an endless supply of mince pies. I liked the work in the English bakeries, as there was a great deal of variety, and I got on quite well with English employers. I was often slagged for not going to the pub or meeting the lads after work. That probably helped to distance them further from me, and in many ways I lost out as far as making friends was concerned.

I had already tried a long sea voyage, with a working trip in 1964 to Canada on the *Irish Larch*. We ran into a force 12 storm as the *Larch* entered the great St Lawrence River. The crew were tossed about like empty cartons, and many, including myself, were injured. I ended up in hospital in Bay Como with twenty stitches in a head wound, which left me with a lasting memory of the frightening sound of the wind at sea. It was an experience that made me nervous of long sea voyages.

I began to wonder if I had made the right decision. Much of the voyage would be in bad weather, which had me feeling very apprehensive.

With less than a week to go, I was on the night shift in Emilio's. It was a Saturday morning, and I was feeling quite ill. As I prepared to go home, I felt dizzy. I walked home that cold frosty morning through the old cobbled streets of Bradford and wondered, what now!

I could see the Valley footbal ground and the frosty rooftops of the terraced houses, blackened by years of smoke from the factories and the mills.

The landlady greeted me warmly, as usual, as did her mother, both of whom were Irish. Her husband, Frank, who came from Crumlin in Dublin, worked in the office at the bakery, where he made up the wages. At breakfast I overheard them say how ill I looked. When Frank sat down opposite me I was anxious to know for certain. 'Frank—do I look okay to you?' He grinned as he looked up at me. His mind was on his bacon and eggs. Pointing his fork, he said, 'If you can eat fry-ups, Pat, then you're as well as I am.' But I wondered.

Frank glanced at me, taking his eye off the food. 'Don't take too much heed of them women. They'd have you dying before you go to the grave.' They all laughed.

I couldn't wait to get to bed, as I felt washed up. New

Zealand was far from my mind as I entered the bathroom. Without warning there was a flash of light. I had hit the bathroom floor. For a while there were stars, then light, and finally darkness.

When I woke up I was in Bradford Royal Infirmary, with smiling nurses looking down at me. I was shocked, and utterly confused. I began to shout and scream. 'Oh, God, this isn't true. It's a nightmare! Let me go now!' The nurses quickly calmed me down.

The doctor was a small young man with a Scottish accent. 'What's wrong with me, doctor? I'm due to sail to New Zealand soon. I've paid for the trip.' 'Well, Patrick, we've got good news and bad news. You're to be with us for some time.' My heart sank. I began to think of Jersey and the awful experience I had had to endure, and now here I was again. I forced back the tears as I waited for the doctor to explain what was wrong with me. 'You'll have to forget your travels for some time. I'm sorry, Patrick, but you can consider yourself lucky. You could have been at sea. You have an inflamed ulcer, a small duodenal, which is just below your stomach.' As I looked about the room, I got the impression everyone was watching me. The doctor finished by saying, 'Well, instead of spending Christmas in the sun out in New Zealand, our nurses in the Bradford Royal will see to it that you enjoy every minute of your stay here. The treatment will start tomorrow, Patrick, and you will be six to eight weeks with us, then three further months on treatment as an out-patient.'

When the day arrived on which I had been due to sail from Southampton, I was afraid to open my eyes. I simply did not want to see anyone.

I began to have constant nightmares. One morning I woke up with my pillow held closely to me—in another ward, lying beneath a bed! I'd been dreaming I was chased by the Sheriff in Artane and was hiding beneath Quickfart's bed. When I woke up I realised I was in a female ward. I managed to get out before being noticed.

In times of stress I always got dreams of my past; whenever I was contented, the nightmares ceased. Once when I was being awakened for breakfast the nurse was amazed to find that I was in bed with my clothes on. When the staff nurse was informed she put two and two together. 'Walking in your sleep again, Patrick? I'll change the pills for you.' She added, 'He'll walk out one of these nights and get run down!'

Christmas Eve in 1967 in Bradford Royal Infirmary brought my entire past experience back to me. As the doors of the ward opened, two rows of nurses with lighted candles came in, singing Christmas carols. To me they looked like angels in their red cloaks, so full of grace and beauty. By the time the sixty nurses, matrons and doctors had finished singing 'Hark, the Herald Angels Sing', I was filled with joy. At that moment the awful cloud of loneliness lifted. With all the love and care, I felt I was at home. And yet this was England. I had been taught as a child that the English were evil. I never thought that they could be like this, so kind, so beautifully organised. A staff nurse placed a card on my locker; it read, *Get well soon, Larry. Love, Helen.*

AFTER ALMOST SEVEN weeks in the Bradford Royal, I decided to return to Ireland. The night work, the long hours and bad eating habits had taken their toll. I would have to be more careful, and I promised the nurses and doctors I would be.

On the flight home my emotions almost got the better of me. After a cup of tea I began to feel somewhat better, but I knew I had a long way to go to be back to my own best form. I became frightened, not fully knowing where I would put my head down or in whose house I would be staying. Home to me was wherever I unpacked my suitcase. It was a lonely thought, and for the first time I realised since leaving Artane that I had no fixed abode.

I dozed off. My thoughts brought me back to the autumn evening in Marino in 1960 when I answered a knock on the door. I was shocked to see a face from my past: it was

Brother Simon from Artane. I held open the door as Molly shouted, 'Let him in, Pat, he's going to stay for a few weeks.' Simon, who was to share my room, explained to me why he left the Christian Brothers, how he fell in love with a beautiful young woman whom he met by chance while on duty in Artane one Sunday, out for the usual Sunday walk.

Simon only came to Artane on summer relief in the early fifties. He was a good-looking man, though too nice, I thought, for that life. I wondered how he coped with being married after leading such a sheltered life.

I thought of summer in St Brelade's—of the girl I left behind, only to be deserted by her. Oh, God, what kind of fool am I? Then thoughts of Helen from Bingley flooded my heart. I was becoming depressed, lovesick, deprived of the little things that most people take for granted: home, and all the joys of home; a mother's love—the things that seem too small to notice until it's too late.

I tried to think of where I would sleep that night. Mrs Mooney's words came back to me: 'A rolling stone collects no moss, Pat. You need to settle somewhere and have roots.' I wondered where I would work and what I would do, as I was only a baker, and night work was killing me. I longed for a really decent break. 'Just one, dear God,' I begged. 'Just one.'

14

The Shadow of Artane

Carmella O'Grady offered me a room in her house in Anglesea Road, Ballsbridge. After my long stay in Bradford Royal Infirmary I reckoned I could do with some home cooking. But for some reason I declined the offer; and then when I was about to phone her and accept, I was offered lodgings and a job in Rathmines.

To my bitter disappointment, the job in Gerrard's Bakery went badly for me. It was a hard place to work in. Obviously I wasn't up to it, and the lads didn't know my background. I found I was getting very irritated with workmates. It was a strictly non-union bakery, and I found a few of the lads to be either dreadful 'licks' or too downright inquisitive and pushy for my liking. I was never one for asking lads for their complete history just because I found myself working with them. I was also at fault because of my knowledge of the mixture and texture of a dough. I was very well experienced in the art of knowing when a cake or a batch of bread or buns was baked—without going to the oven every five minutes to check, as so many managers do.

So many problems arose with lads forever wanting to be in charge without first having a sound background knowledge of what it was they were so anxious to take charge of. Regularly I found myself working under managers and foremen who seemed to chance their arm and put in for a position as a bakery manager, then to start picking the brains of decent workers. These types got on in such places as non-union bakeries; they would never have made their mark in a union house, without proving their ability first.

After some months I became somewhat depressed. Perhaps it was frustration and, more to the heart of the matter, the fact that I was always earning very low wages for very hard work, especially night work and very early morning work—for no extra money. I began to hate work.

I moved from Gerrard's because of a bit of a punch-up I had with the boss. I had been asked to put a box of fat into the doughnut frier by the boss. I looked at the boxes of fats and hurriedly asked a chap who came by if it was the right fat, as I was not familiar with them at all: some of the fats being used were far superior to others in the making of cakes. I was handed a box of unmarked fat and put it into the frier, and bingo!—what a mess!

I roared laughing as I stood there watching the fat rise in the hot frier like a volcanic eruption, as did the chap who handed me the fat. The boss came towards us with a shocked look on his face. I tried to explain what had happened, but couldn't hide my laughter at the incredible mess it made on the floor. I told him how I had used the wrong fat. 'I know that, you bloody ape!' He moved towards me. I was sure he was going to hit me, so I drew out and punched him on the jaw. He quickly struck me in return, and I ended up in hospital for the day. I was shocked to learn that he had not been going to strike me at all, but by then it was too late.

My flat at the time was on the third floor of a three-storey house in Rathmines. I began meeting girls, and I was allowed to bring them in. The landlady was a warm-hearted Tipperary woman. Her husband was a civil servant, a very tall, straight man, too fond of the drink and an ardent Catholic. Often I joined him in their living-room to say the Rosary at night, whenever I had no date or visitors.

One evening I dropped in to see them. It was about ten o'clock—their prayer time. I noticed he was not there, and then I was ushered out by the landlady. She looked very bothered. Suddenly I heard shouting as I walked up the stairs. 'It's him!' I stayed a moment to listen. I was shocked and amused at his crazy notions. 'You were with him again, Mary. I don't trust that new lodger of yours at all now. He's been seeing you. Tell me or I'll go up and drag him down here.' I heard his wife shout at him. 'You're drunk, you fool, as usual. You're not half the man he is. I swear to God on it, and he so young. Look at you, a bloody civil servant—a drunken lout, bedad!' I hurried up to my flat and bolted the door.

Suddenly there was a knock, then a whispering. 'Are you in, Pat? Pat!' I opened the door. She spoke hurriedly. This could only happen to me, I thought. 'You must lock your door and put whatever furniture you can against it—quickly. Have you got any girls with you?' I laughed at the question. 'No. What a pity. None at all. No-one loves me, Mary, any more.' She blushed and began to warn me of her husband. 'He's dangerous. We have a problem. He's an alcoholic, and he's drunk and angry. He thinks you and I are seeing each other. You must leave here in the morning. I have a safe house for you to go to in Castle Avenue.'

How could he think such a thing? I heard him shout up at her. 'I'll kill him! I'm coming up!' I closed the door and put all the furniture against it. I heard her shout, 'I'm calling the Guards. They'll fix you, you mad drunken fool.'

As I sat waiting to see what was going to happen, a hatchet came through the door. He roared in at me. 'I'll get to you, lover boy. I've never trusted Dublin lodgers in my life or in my house. Say the Rosary with my wife, do yeh? I'll say a decade over your dead body for yeh! Let me in!'

He smashed down the door of the flat, and I had to hold him off. He was over six feet tall. He pushed me, then swung the hatchet down at me. I sidestepped, and as I grabbed hold of him, the guards arrived. He held me by the throat and I was really struggling at that point. His wife was shouting to me, 'Hit him! Kill him! Kill him!' The guards then led him away. I followed them downstairs, and watched as he faced his wife in the hall. He swore at her. 'I was right, Mary, all the while. I knew he wasn't coming in to say the Rosary with you. Oh, no, Mary, you were seeing him also.'

I was found new lodgings at two that morning, and I moved into my new bedsitter in Castle Avenue. I felt I had been involved in a nightmare.

Later I took a walk to find my way and to see where I was living, as I wanted to get to know the area. I came across a bakery and confectionery shop; I looked up at the name, which read *W. Ferguson and Sons*. I thought I'd try my luck for a job. Ten minutes later I walked out smiling. I was to start at eight next morning. The money was fine: sixteen pounds ten a week, including a fully cooked breakfast, dinner and tea every day. I was over the moon.

Ferguson's was a lovely place to work in. I loved getting up in the mornings to go to work, and I learnt quite a bit about confectionery and cake mixing there.

A strange thing happened a few weeks later. The boss took a call from Artane School, from the Brother in charge of settling boys when they were sixteen. Mr Ferguson called me into his little office, which was beneath the stairs leading to the famous Ferguson's Tea Rooms. He sat me down and began to explain that my old school had requested that we take a boy, if not two, and train them, as the school was to close down as an industrial boarding school by the summer. I took a deep breath. For a moment there was silence. I was about to leave when he added, 'By the way, I may need you to come with me.' As I hurried home that evening I felt the shadow of my past engulf me. Why me? I thought.

Mr Ferguson called me in again a few days later. 'I'm going to ask you to go up to Artane with me, or with my son if I can't make it. I've decided to take a boy off their hands and give him a good training. If he works out, then I may take a second. We need you, Patrick, to help us out and to help us choose the right kind. I hear Brother O'Connor has quite a few orphan boys on his hands who have to be fixed up, as they hope to close by June.'

The trip brought back memories I had long since forgotten. As the car turned up the Malahide Road, within minutes I could see Marino Christian Brothers' School, and then the dark dreary buildings of Artane School, which so dominated the whole area of Donnycarney and Artane, as they do to this day.

As the car turned to go up the main avenue, my heart beat faster and my hands were sweaty. The boss drove slowly up the avenue. He looked surprised at the neatness of the grounds and at how big the place was. Once out of the car they were both astonished at the size of the buildings, and wanted to know what they were all for.

I noticed Brother Joe O'Connor coming down the steps of the office. I could see he was delighted we came. He remembered me well as I introduced him to my boss. It was at that point I got the feeling I had never left—yet here I was, about to choose an orphan lad to come and learn a trade with us.

I stood inside the infirmary, which had been turned into a small dormitory, and I was really taken aback: the rows of beds so neatly made up; the centre aisle glittering up at me; the statue of Our Lady and the holy water font.

I could clearly imagine it all. I was sure I could hear the cries of the boys being flogged. It all came back to me. In many ways it was a blessing, being asked to go there, as my past had to come out into the open, and it reminded me of what my childhood was really about. In so many ways it was an extraordinary childhood, I thought, as I stared silently over at the boys.

They were neatly dressed in their Artane serge cloth, hobnailed boots, and crew-cut hair; and that awful lonesome, hungry appearance brought it all back to me. Ten years had passed already, although it seemed like only a few months.

I helped to choose the boy. The choice was not a difficult one, as there were only three to pick from who wanted to work in a bakery. I saw this small, tubby, fresh-faced lad with a sad look on his round face. He gave me a slight grin. I

116

could see he was longing for a break and hoping I would choose him. Brother O'Connor gave me a rather dry smile, as though he suspected I was thinking of the time he battered my bottom so badly I thought my buttocks were two lumps of rare meat, and, what's more, I knew he enjoyed every second of it.

When I got home to my flat in Castle Avenue I was drained in so many ways. I lay down and closed my eyes. All I could think of was my past.

But by the end of 1968 change was on the way, in the form of value-added tax. My boss didn't like it at all, and then I heard it from the man himself. 'Time to get out. Too much tax, too many costs, and too little profit.' Ferguson's was to close the following year. I felt I had been struck a mortal blow.

ABOUT THIS TIME I saw an advertisement for a car going very cheaply. I called to the flat in Leinster Road, Rathmines, to see it. Who should answer the doorbell only the bold Quickfart himself. We chatted for what seemed like hours in his bedsitter. I gave him all the news I had—including what happened to me in London. When he heard he hit the roof with laughter. 'Did you ever meet Oxo Ryan on your travels, Paddy?' he asked me. 'As a matter of fact I did. He worked in Lyon's in London,' I told him.

He just talked and talked, about Artane in general and about Oxo. Some of the memories were painful for him. He became angry and upset telling me about what Oxo had been through. He showed me a photograph he had of him. Suddenly I glanced at my watch and shouted, 'Bloody hell, I've got to be going. Will you show me the car? Maybe you'll let me have it very reasonable?' I smiled at him. I was hoping to get his mind off his past. 'Come on, Quickie, I'd like to test-drive that car.'

He stood, shrugged his broad shoulders, and agreed. I bought the car from him for about £160. 'You know where to find me Paddy, if it breaks down.' I enjoyed a good laugh at that one, as he moved about more than even I did. As I drove away from Leinster Road, a strange thought entered my mind that one day I could write a book about Oxo Ryan and his fantastic escapes.

Lads like Oxo were drawn over the bog at dawn and stripped to their shorts and forced to run around the yard at six in the morning, and whipped by the Feeler each time they passed him. It had all come back to me. I was once in Oxo's gang in 1954. It was the time of his last escape plan at the Corpus Christi procession. It went well, and poor Oxo went to England, never to return. He broke ranks as we marched by the poultry farm singing 'Faith of Our Fathers'. I smiled then at that lovely thought, just as I did all those years ago when Oxo made his final bid for freedom.

For some reason I believed Quickfart knew where Oxo was now. I wondered if they were still in contact with each other. Perhaps he's home living in Dublin and married? The more I thought of the photograph, the more I was inclined to believe he was.

15

Bon Voyage

Lavinia was slim with a very dark complexion and extremely black hair. She grew up not too far from the Dublin foothills, beyond Taylor's Grange. She spoke with a warm, educated Dublin accent. For the first time I dated a girl who owned a car.

Lavinia worked as a doctor's secretary in a city hospital. Her parents ran a small but busy newsagents. She showered me with small gifts from the shop. Although I had my own flat and was well fed in Ferguson's Tea Rooms, at the weekends I catered for myself, and the small gifts of various foods came in useful for both of us. I found Lavinia to be quite a different kind of girl from any I had previously dated. She seemed to make all the decisions, and was quick to tell me what I could and could not wear while on a date.

My flat was like a second home to her. I was trying not to fall in love with her, as my passage to New Zealand was again booked and paid for. I wanted more than anything else to travel the world on a beautiful ocean liner. I knew I couldn't make plans for the future with Lavinia once I had learnt that Ferguson's would close. Lavinia was trying to get me to change my plans. She had started to convince me how much she needed me, and I began to believe she might be in love with me.

On the night of her twenty-fourth birthday she was to call

around to my place in Castle Avenue at half seven, and from there we were going out for dinner, to a place of her choice. I was having a wash and shave when I heard the door opening then closing. I could smell the beautiful warm fragrance. I was shaving as she came behind me. I shouted, 'I won't be long. Give me a minute.' I was standing in my bare feet with just a pair of shorts on. It was a hot night, towards the end of July. Suddenly, without warning, I felt her hands around my waist, and my shorts were off. I said, 'Hold it, will you! Just a second till I get finished.' Her voice was velvety soft. 'I know what you need, darling, and I will hold it—I promise you.' I froze as she carried out her promise.

'Can I turn on the radiogram, Pat?' she asked. I agreed, of course. 'The records are all of Joan Baez.' 'What will I play for you?' she asked. '"All My Trials, Love".' She responded swiftly. 'Oh, you poor soul. I'd love to hear about your trials. You seem to me to be a lonesome poor soul in need of love.' 'Well, in that case, as it's your birthday, Lavinia, play the other side of that record—you'll like it: "Plaisir d'Amour".' I sat up and smiled at her. She placed it on the turntable and lay down beside me. Her voice was soft. 'So you are a romantic after all, Pat. Anyone I know who collects the music of Joan Baez is a romantic dreamer de luxe.' Her lips met mine in a swift, passionate embrace.

I was on a high that lasted for about six weeks. I was convinced she loved me—yet I found it difficult to think at all. I had decided to ask her to marry me, certain she would agree. I wasn't disappointed, and I brought her out to meet the O'Gradys. Carine and her mother liked her; I was delighted. 'Where ever did you meet her, Patrick?' Carine asked, and quickly added, 'She does seem awfully nice, Patrick—can you afford her?' I just laughed, knowing bloody well I couldn't.

Everything was going so well it was too good to be true. I had a chance meeting with Mando in the city centre. He looked as neatly dressed as ever. 'You still go to the pawn office and the dress hire for your clothes?' I asked him. He smiled. 'What do you think, Paddy? I'd never get clothes like this working in the Home Bakery.' 'Yes, I know, Mando. The reason I ask you is, I wonder could you help me get some nice gear?' He latched on quickly. 'Oh, you got hitched, Paddy. Goin' to marry her then?' I was glad he asked. 'Well, I'd like to. Could you help me out?'

'Help you out? Of course! Come on, me oul' flower, I'll treat you to a one-and-one.'

I sat down in the Rainbow Rooms in O'Connell Street with him and, as usual, he got a loan of a few pounds from me. 'What's she like?' he asked me with a grin. I smiled and said, 'Very special. She's agreed to marry me.' He almost knocked over a chair. 'Paddy, yeh've cracked it! 'Member the night yeh blew up the bakery? I was teachin' yeh to waltz. Yeh bleedin' nearly killed us both, Paddy, that night.' 'How could I ever forget,' I said, as I kept glancing at my watch, trying to give him a hint.

Shortly after we said goodbye I was walking past the Metropole cinema when I caught sight of Lavinia. As I was about to approach her, a short, stocky man put his arm around her, and she responded with a long kiss on his lips. As the queue began to move, she looked up and noticed me watching her. All this while I had thought that she loved me! Oh, God, I could have belted her!

He noticed that she was looking at me, and walked over to me. I was stunned at the roughness of his voice. He swore at me, and reached out his hand either to wave me away or, as I thought, push me off. I wasn't thinking. I drew out and hit him in the mouth. Suddenly I was floored: I never saw the karate kick coming. As I lay on the ground I could hear Lavinia shout, 'Oh, come on, Raymond—leave it be. He's past tense now.' He came towards me and swore at me. 'You fuckin' well go near my bird again, mate, and I'll kick your head in.' He began to go for me as I got to my feet. Lavinia shouted, 'Leave him, Ray—he's useless.'

I was standing just a few feet from him and I could clearly see his sour, hardened features. 'Keep away from my fiancée or I'll break your neck.' I felt I had to respond to him while she was just a few feet away. 'You can have your bird, mate, feathered or unfeathered. I wouldn't go near her with a barge-pole.' I knew I'd said too much but I stood my ground. He came for me, but Lavinia caught hold of his arm. She shouted and screamed, 'Let him go, Ray.' His mouth was bloodied; I watched him spit out. He looked viciously towards me. Lavinia became angry and raised her voice. 'Let him go. If you don't, I'll go home, I promise.' He raised his finger to my face, making more threats as Lavinia pulled him away.

I was shaken, yet in a way relieved that I had seen it all with my own eyes. I reckoned I deserved the last word. I shouted as she hauled him away towards the cinema, 'She's all yours, mate. You deserve each other.' I was at a loss for better words, as she suddenly turned around and gave me the two-fingered sign. I knew then that she was no good.

I was glad I had my passage booked to New Zealand. I was alone again.

In August 1970 the boss told me that the bakery would close within six months, and he told me I was doing the right thing in going to New Zealand. I believed strongly that I was, and decided that even if I got homesick I would stay at least twelve months and see a bit of the world before returning.

I had a few days' holidays, and my thoughts now went back to Barnacullia. I made my way up Grange Road, Rathfarnham, in the old car I had bought a few months earlier from Quickfart. As I got to Taylor's Grange and turned left towards Sandyford, I was shocked to see Lavinia. She came over to me—all smiles!

'Hello, how are you keeping yourself, Pat?' I was silent and remained by the car. It took a few moments for what was happening to soak in. She stood very close to me; I could smell her sweet breath and her perfume. I moved to get back into the car. As I opened the door, I heard her say, rather invitingly, 'You going for a drive in that thing?' I was tempted for a moment, but didn't want to get involved. I climbed into the car, and was surprised to see her open the passenger door and smile in at me. 'Hey, you going for a drive on your own? You not inviting me along?' Her smile and tempting ways were too much for me. 'Okay, hop in then. You win, Lavinia.'

She was full of self-confidence, as always. 'I always get what I want, and let go when I've had enough of it. I've always liked you, Pat, and what's more I still do, but I'm not ready for your ideas of being married and staying at home to keep house for you while you're working in some kip of a bakery. I wouldn't be able to stand that sort of life. You'd have to get a better job for a start. I like you, Pat, but I couldn't love someone who has a rotten job—know what I mean?' All the while I was longing to get beneath her blouse.

We drove through Stepaside, which brought back fond memories. I felt her hand on my shoulder. 'Pull up over there. Look, in that lay-by.' As I did, my pulse raced. I cast my pride to the breeze and let out all the lustful passion that was driving me wild.

I had seen girls' breasts before, but none so inviting as Lavinia's, and she was very proud of them. She was wearing a loose red v-shaped blouse but no bra. Her lips were filled with passion, inviting me to taste her sweet breath. Our lips found each other as she teased and tempted me. Then after a moment and very distinctly she said, 'I'm a virgin, and I have a doctor's letter to prove it.' I almost caved in. God, what would Mando have thought of that, I wondered!

THE *SHOTA RUSTAVELI* was a Russian liner, and I was one of two thousand people from Ireland, England, Malta and Cyprus on board. My first impression of the huge ship when I arrived in Southampton was of its enormous size. It was spotless, and when I walked up the gangway into the shining corridors I felt as if I was in a hospital! For the five weeks I was on board, the great liner was like an incredible floating city.

My first walk around after I had settled into my cabin,

which was a four-berth, became a walk into another romance—within hours of coming on board! I was getting a breath of fresh air and had watched the English coastline fade slowly into the distance when I noticed a slim, tall young woman coming towards me. She had dark shoulder-length hair and was holding a cigarette. She looked at me and smiled. I got a whiff of her perfume and was attracted to her casual, film-star charm and her tantalising smile.

She spoke softly. 'Have you got a match for me?' Bloody hell! I never seem to have anything they need. 'I'm so sorry, I don't smoke,' I said apologetically. She put away the cigarette.

'My name is Andrea. I'm from New Zealand.' Her hand was outstretched and mine reached slowly to hold it as I introduced myself. What fine long fingers, I thought. I held on to her hand, as she wasn't letting go. I felt at ease. We were alone on deck, and we both stood staring at the distant coastline. I imagined I was dreaming. She soon convinced me otherwise.

Andrea turned and began to move along the deck. I followed with a certain reluctance, not sure of myself. Then she paused, long enough for me to catch up. I began to feel this could be my lucky day—and all this in the first few hours. It did strike me as something of a fantasy.

We were now in a short darkened passageway, and the only sound was from the seagulls. My hand seemed to rest lightly at first around her waist. 'Tell me about New Zealand, Andrea.' 'It's quite a beautiful country, and it's now the start of summer there.' Her voice became a soft, warm whisper. I was floating on a cloud. 'I'll tell you some more later. We have over four weeks to go, you know.' Her lips closed in upon mine. Her long fingers rested in my hair. Losing any clear notions I had in respect of her charm and elegance, I let myself go. I felt like saying, 'I love you, Andrea,' but I thought there was no urgent need. We had over four weeks at sea, and I wouldn't make such a foolish statement, as love comes all too soon.

As our lips parted, I knew by her that she would go to any lengths to be pleased. Her smooth, long hands eased their way along the flat of my stomach. Goodness, I thought, there's no need for me to prolong my quest for love. Could this last? I could feel every inch of her slender body. Her lips pressed tightly over mine. I couldn't breathe, but what the hell.

A light came on that brightened up the passageway. I noticed a huge deckhand, then another. I helped Andrea to her feet; she was shocked to see them so close. They passed some comment and then roared with laughter. 'Come on, Andrea, I'll see you back to your cabin.'

Before she went I could at last see how she really looked in the bright light. I was overwhelmed by her attractiveness. Her voice would have melted ice. 'Can I share your table in the dining-room for the voyage?' she asked. I was alone and would have to sit either at a table for six or a table for two. We had a table for two for the entire voyage. However, Andrea did not inform me when she would come for meals, and sometimes, especially mornings, she would miss out.

The trip to New Zealand was more of an adventure than a sea voyage. When the *Shota Rustaveli* reached the Panama Canal, I went with a few English people from the ship in search of a supermarket in the Canal Zone, which was under American rule. The heat on board ship had been bad, but when we left it to go into the town, it was something else. I had difficulty walking and even breathing.

Once inside the store I got a glimpse of Andrea, who was with a few girls from her cabin. I made my way towards her. Just as I reached her a row broke out: an American service-man stopped Andrea and her friends from purchasing goods they had chosen. Without thinking, I rushed over to them and faced the Americans, who had their guns at the ready. One of them shouted at us to get out of the store at once or there would be trouble. Then the serviceman repeated the warning with a change: 'English out of the store, please—at once.' After a brief silence he shouted, 'All passengers of the Russian ship leave the store.'

Suddenly he began to push the girls. I walked out in front of him. I shouted, 'I'm Irish. Some of these people are from New Zealand, mate.' Within seconds we were all hounded out of the store. I hurried back to face up to one of them. He looked so clean-cut and neat, but very macho. I shouted, 'We're not going, you know.' A voice came over the loud-speaker system and warned all people from the Russian liner to go back to the ship and remain there at once. Someone came towards me and advised me to follow him back, as the ship was under arrest!

We were repeatedly stopped by American reporters and asked what the crew looked like and how they treated us, what the food was like, and if we could get what we wanted to eat. I was asked if there were any KGB men on board! The whole thing was like some mixed-up nightmare.

On the third day in Panama the captain announced that we were about to leave this friendly American port. The cheer that went up surprised even the crew.

I WAS INVITED by a senior member of the crew, on behalf of Club Travel, to meet the head chef and show him how to make up plain Irish and English dishes, such as salads, with chips, and how to serve a plain cooked breakfast. I was also invited to demonstrate the making of white yeast bread, brown bread, and scones. I was stunned by the stony silence I got from the crew as I showed them my way of baking bread. I stood frozen to the floor as the galley crew stared blankly at me.

I demonstrated to them how I made apple pie and scones, but they wanted me to make biscuits for them. They brought over some of their own Russian biscuits for me to sample. They were awful!

Then I was offered a drink. As it looked like a glass of water, I was happy to take it with a smile. The crew remained silent. I raised my glass to them. The chef urged me to swallow quickly in one swift gulp, as was their custom. I downed the drink to roars of laughter and shouts, and then I was on the floor. I had swallowed a full glass of 100 per cent Russian vodka. I could see the crew going round and round about me. My stomach was in hell.

I woke up the following morning, naked in my bunk, covered in very sticky Russian marmalade, my private parts covered in royal icing. I got a message to visit the ship's surgery, and there I had to face up to the crazy job of getting the icing off, with the help of a Russian nurse. I was well warned after that episode about how the Russians like to have fun, and rough fun at that.

WHEN THE DAY came for crossing the Equator, I was one of the dozen chosen—without being informed—for the ceremony and blessing by King Neptune. I was simply asked not to come up to the swimming pool neatly dressed, and if I was attending to wear shorts and nothing else. I looked at the man who invited me. He had a suspicious look on his big round face. His English was not bad, I thought, for a Russian. I suspected that something was about to happen on deck at three that afternoon, but exactly what, to whom and how, I had no idea.

At half two I wandered about the outer deck and moved along the huge crowd. I noticed Andrea and made my way towards her. She was wearing a two-piece yellow and black swimsuit. Suddenly we were surrounded by five or six fierce-looking Russian crewmen. Andrea didn't seem put out that the big hulks were tight against her and me, but I was concerned. The music started, trumpets at first, then a roll of the drums. I looked towards the main platform. 'Look,' I said, pointing to a huge man coming towards the platform, wearing a crown with horns, a long beard, and a cloak of fur that dragged along behind him, and holding a long implement with three spears on top. The roll of drums got louder as it was announced that he was King Neptune.

He proceeded to read out a list of passengers who, they said, 'have since the voyage began broken the following rules of the speedy ship *Shota Rustaveli*, laid down by Neptune.' Suddenly my name was mentioned. 'That Patrick Laurence Touher failed to do the garden, as his early morning duty required him to do ... for hanging out of his porthole a pair of dirty underwear ... for being seen kissing a young woman passenger in a private place ... for complaining to the purser about our very wonderful Russian food ... for refusing a glass of pure Russian vodka ... For that he also receives ten lashes after being cleansed and sanctified in the waters of the Black Sea.' I was instantly surrounded, lifted off my feet, and carried over the heads of the passengers to stand before Neptune. I got a glimpse of Andrea being hauled along the deck and put beside me.

To a roll of the drums I was pushed over a stool in front of Neptune and, with my shorts pulled down, my buttocks were rubber-stamped with blue dye. I received the ten lashes, which I never felt, although the sound was most authentic. Then I was lifted high in the air by the two strong crewmen and dropped into the waters of the Black Sea (i.e. the swimming pool). I hit the water, which was a good twenty feet below, like a ton of cement. I sank to the bottom, but was lifted out of the water at once. All the people who were packed around the huge pool were cheering as I was carried, now cleansed and sanctified, and placed before the throne. To a roll of drums I was given the drink of peace and forgiveness. To be precise, my head was pulled back by an ape of a man while another, who was dressed like a bear, poured vodka and some other concoction down my throat.

I was shocked to see them pull down Andrea's swimsuit to reveal her breasts, then to rubber-stamp them with a big plunger, colouring them and later her bare buttocks with blue dye. They then poured a bucket of awful-looking slime over her, while Neptune read out her sins. One was for not being generous with the crew ... for not wearing a nightie in her cabin ... for not wearing a see-through swimsuit while acting in *South Pacific*. Then she too was tossed into the pool.

LIFE ABOARD THE ship was fantastic. I took part in stage shows, the best of them *South Pacific*. Andrea took a big part in that.

They organised a poetry reading, with pride of place for anyone who recited their own poetry. I was driven to write at that time, so I entered for the reading, which was to be held in the great dining-room after the evening dinner, as a form of cabaret.

I strolled the decks at night in the humid Pacific air, and wondered if I was in the real world at all or a world of make-believe. I was a super-romantic and a sentimentalist, but I loved it all. Beats going into a hovel of a bakery at two in the morning, I thought.

I was writing poetic trash. It was simply like writing love letters, only to read them over and say to myself, 'Imagine I wrote that!' and laugh before tearing it up. But I did manage to write a few real poems on that incredible journey to New Zealand.

On the night of the poetry reading Andrea came to dinner with me. She wanted to hear my poems. She looked beautiful in her red dress with a blue silk sash around her waist. Her smile simply radiated confidence and encouragement for me as my name was called out. I was either being honoured or being disposed of quickly—I wasn't sure which—but I was the first to perform. I had to stand on stage before two thousand people, the captain, the officers and crew and hear the host describe me as a new Irish poet who was going to recite his own newly written poems, specially written in the last few hours for the occasion. The applause was ear-shattering. I took out my first poem, called 'Some Mother's Son'. It's about a young man washed up on the sands at the end of the Second World War, whom I learnt of while on my first visit to the Isle of Man in 1959. I followed that by reading 'The Coal Fire', for which I received a rapturous applause.

I tried to leave the stage, but everybody stood up and began chanting for more, and I was led back. I tried to get a glimpse of Andrea, and when I spotted her I felt fine. I wanted her to hear the poem I wrote with her in mind and dedicated to her, 'The MS *Shota Rustaveli*'.

FROM THE MOMENT I got up at around nine every morning until I went to my cabin for the night between midnight and two, there was always something for me to do. Each morning I took charge of the keep-fit fanatics' class at half ten. There was a writers' workshop at noon. One-act plays were performed at night in the main lounge in front of over five hundred people, and I took part in these too.

After lunch there were sports, from basketball to clay pigeon shooting. There were three small cinemas, which showed the very best films. There was also a choice of bars, lounges, dancing, cabaret, and stage shows. I was eager to participate in all the sports and shows, and in this way I was always kept active.

WHEN WE ARRIVED in Auckland, the sun was extremely hot. I was dressed in a pure wool three-piece suit, and I was stared at as I walked down the gangway. God, I muttered, how am I going to stick this heat? Andrea came towards me, and once again I blew it—as always! I felt she had ignored me at times to be with other men friends at night in clubs and at the roulette tables. I thought she was simply using me to suit herself. However, it is a custom of New Zealand and Australian women to be wined and dined by several men in one evening and even at one party. It was not my style and I would never accept that strange custom, but God, how I loved her. Yet my foolish heart said no again!

16

Strange Customs

When Andrea asked me if I had a place to stay, I felt cold and distant towards her, though in my heart I loved her dearly. Her dark hazel eyes were reading my mind. 'Would you like to come and stay in my home down in Palmerstown? You're most welcome.'

I looked at her, and without really giving it a second thought I said, 'I'll stay in Auckland. After all, I've come twelve thousand miles to be here. I'll find some place to stay.' She looked sad as she silently went on her way. Little did I realise that I would never again see the beautiful New Zealand girl who had stolen my heart in the first hours of the long voyage.

Afterwards I felt lost, lonesome and foolish as I settled in to my room in the YMCA hostel in the city, with my thoughts and my dreams shattered by a few moments of foolishness, which I couldn't put right. I must admit that down through the years I have made some dreadful decisions that later left me sick with self-pity.

There were times when I wanted to end it all, and once I actually tried. I was out along the beach at Bream Bay, and I was feeling so homesick that I would have offered everything I owned for the sound of an Irish voice, while a piece of Irish music on the radio had me in tears. I walked into the water from the golden stretch of sand. I simply wanted to keep on walking, when I took a fall over some rocks beneath the water. I fell head down onto the rocks, which were close to a giant coral reef. I heard a voice shouting, 'You okay out there, mate?' Within moments I was lifted out to the safety of the reef, with blood oozing from a head wound. I opened my eyes to find a young woman cleaning my wounds with the help of her boy-friend. I was taken by surprise when I realised she was topless!

He was quick to apologise. His accent was a mixture of Yorkshire and New Zealand. 'Sorry, mate, for the way we're dressed, or undressed.' He smiled. 'We come here at weekends and swim out to the reef like this—as quite a lot of us do in these parts.' He looked at his girl-friend and said, 'This is Jean. She comes from a place near Te-Aroha, near Morrinsville.' He shook my hand. 'I'm Erin.' Odd name, I thought, and smiled. Blood was getting into my eyes and I felt dizzy. I just heard him say, 'I've got an Irish passport,' and then I passed out.

I had a good nurse looking after me in Jean. I was brought back to their house near Wellsford, where I stayed for a few days. Jean was a teacher with first aid experience. She was the kind of girl I dreamed of ending up with.

I FOUND IT almost impossible to sleep at night. It was then I finally realised how far away from Croke Park I was. Those buzzards called mosquitoes kept me awake most nights. My body was sucked by the noisy beggars for about ten weeks, and for the remainder of that summer I slept beneath a mosquito net.

Once I had a nightmare in the lodging house I had moved into in Ponsonby, near Grey Lynn, a large suburb just at the top end of Auckland. I woke up to find I was tangled in the mosquito net like a fly trapped in a spider's web. The gentle knocking on the door told me it was Angelina coming to do my room. I shouted, 'Please close the door, for God's sake.' I could hear her laughter. 'I've been trapped for hours in this

My bakery days in Ferguson's.

Mother and child: Pauline and baby daughter, Paula.

That's me playing the tuba in a summer performance in Malahide Castle with St Patrick's Brass and Reed Band, Balbriggan.

As a baker in a Dublin city hot shop, taking sponge cakes from the oven.

The soccer referee.

Brother and sister coming up from the sea.

John, Paula, Suzanne and Pauline, 1989.

Paula's graduation from Dundalk RTC.

Frank Carson with the Touher family.

At the launch in John D.'s: I'm talking to Con O'Connor. On the left are Stephen Lawless and Brian Purcell of Balbriggan Town Commissioners; on the right is Town Clerk, Pat Gibbons.

At the launch of *Fear of the Collar*: Tom and Elma Young with Frank Carson and children.

The Touher family at home.

Pauline and the children down by the sea.

At home with Pauline, working on a draft of *Free As a Bird*.

bloody net. Get me out, will you?' She sat down on my bed laughing.

Angelina was in her late twenties, and helped her mother in the lodging house. She looked half Maori, but her mother was English. Angelina was not an attractive young woman by any means, though her dark complexion took some of the plainness away from her. I was shocked as she cut the net to get me out only to throw her two arms around me, and I fell backwards onto the bed. Angelina was on top of me. Out of the frying pan and into the fire! I had a fight on my hands to get from beneath Angelina. When she held my privates I just screamed. Angelina took flight.

I OPENED LAURENCE'S Home Bakery with a small reception for business and local people, once I had received my diploma and could start. I was unaware of some of New Zealand's customs, and I ran into a few sticky problems. I put on what I thought was a fine spread of food and drink, but as the guests arrived I noticed there was going to be a far bigger crowd than I invited. How was I going to have enough for everyone? Some of the guests I already knew from the voyage. I had kept their addresses and I was glad to meet them again.

How to deal with the Maoris was to be my biggest problem. As I questioned a Maori at the door who was trying to enter the reception with about fifteen of his family, I ran into my first problem with their customs.

I had met Dave on board ship, and he kept in touch. He was a mature young national school teacher, born in New Zealand to English parents. He quickly became my adviser as I tumbled from one problem to the next. He pointed out that when one invites a Maori to a party, they believe they can bring the clan. It doesn't always happen, but in my case I had invited an English lad who was married to a Maori chief's daughter, and she turned up with over fifteen members of their family.

I began to wonder why they had all brought their own

food. I asked Dave, and he pointed out that it was the custom in New Zealand to bring your own 'tucka' and drink to such gatherings. I was left with a hell of a lot of uneaten food.

When a young Maori woman suddenly began to vomit, I moved quickly, like an army officer, to remove her from the premises, thinking this was the correct thing to do. I was quickly approached by a twenty-stone Maori man as I slipped into the kitchen. As he came towards me with what looked like a meat cleaver, he began shouting at me. 'You little man, no-good Englishman, small white arse and small mind with bad tongue! English, I want you. I teach you a lesson you don't forget—see—see!' He came for me, and I began to laugh, although I was terrified. He bashed the cleaver down on the wooden table in the centre of the kitchen. 'You English arsehole. Small man, bad mind, insult my sister and family!' He jumped up and down and then came for me, shouting in Maori.

I began to try and win him over. I was also hoping that someone would come into the kitchen and save me, but we were alone. 'I'm Irish—from Ireland. Don't mean no harm. I'm sorry for hurting you and your sister.'

He took it up wrongly and shouted very loudly, 'You hurt my family of sisters and my woman!' He grabbed hold of me with his iron grip, and laid me out flat on the table. He had me so frightened I couldn't scream. I struggled as he ripped off my shirt. He raised the meat cleaver again. My two hands gripped hold of his arm; it felt like the branch of an oak tree. I tumbled onto the floor. His huge hand took hold of my privates, and I wet my pants, as I was sure he was about to chop them off. Then I passed out.

When I came to I asked Dave to see everyone out, if anyone was still left. I felt I was lucky to be alive and in one piece. I put my hand into my trousers to make sure. The smile Dave's sister, Jennifer, gave me was in itself the answer. 'It's all there,' she said. Then I wondered how she knew!

After Christmas Mass the priest, Father John Davaro, was

outside the church to greet everyone personally. When he came to me his first words were, 'So you're the new man in our parish—just in from the old sod. So tell me, where are you for dinner, Patrick?' I told him, 'I'm alone, father. I've just moved in to the Home Bakery in Ponsonby. It's called Laurence's Home Bakery—formerly Don's Cake Tin.'

'Yes, yes, I know it. Too bad—it's not nice to be left alone at Christmastime for dinner. So you'll come with me to my mother's up in Helensville for a few days? Mother will take care of you. She's a wonderful old lady, Patrick, and she'll simply spoil you, I can tell you now, just to get all the news from home, you see.'

I readily agreed, thrilled that I had someone to talk to for the days ahead. I believed that by keeping up my faith and praying at intervals during the day, good things would really happen and it would help me to settle into my new home. There were times when I wanted some kind of a sheltered life, like Father John. He seemed pleased when I mentioned that to him on the journey through Henderson, where we stopped for a while for him to drop in to visit some old people.

Helensville was out on the coast, east of Auckland Harbour. I loved being brought to new places and meeting as many New Zealanders as possible. Whatever direction I was brought, most of the people seemed to have Irish, English or Scottish connections but had been in New Zealand a long time. I noticed how very relaxed and classless they seemed to be. The girls looked Irish but didn't have the warmth. Far too advanced, I thought!

Christmas Day was a very hot day. I acted as caddy for Father John on the biggest golf course I'd ever seen. I walked miles that day in Helensville, and the spectacular scenery brought home to me that New Zealand was a land of splendid beauty and charm. On the way up to Helensville I noticed that the beaches were crowded.

I smiled as I thought of Ireland. Sunshine was something we expected to come and go, and I realised that there were far more important things in life than golf before Christmas dinner or lying on the hot sands. It all seemed too unreal for me. I began to miss the foggy dew and the frosty winter mornings.

As the weeks passed I became friendly with Frank Quinn and his wife, who ran a small family shop called the Dairy. Frank was from Dublin, and Margaret was from County Tyrone. He was the manager of the Auckland Celtic GAA Club, and I was glad to become a member. Friends of the Quinns soon became friends of mine, and in particular the Hallisseys: Pat, whom I called Pa-Joe, and his lovely sister Brigid. Their parents, who were Irish, were dead, and they had a fine home in Grey Lynn, which was only a few hundred yards from my bakery.

I was having a tough time of it making a living. I soon realised I had made another awful decision. The bakery trade, especially confectionery, which I was doing, was not on: New Zealanders on the whole didn't go in much for cakes or indeed sweet things. Once more I was left cursing my rotten decisions.

I began to make Irish soda bread. The brown soda wouldn't sell, but the Maoris really went for my white bread. However, they soon got fed up buying it. They invited me to the home of a chief, and I was obliged to show them how I made the bread. Soon after that business fell away.

I began to make sausage rolls, pastries, and meat pies, along with birthday and wedding cakes. This was to lead me into a serious problem with a man from Tonga, who lived in a house not far from Pa-Joe and Brigid Hallissey.

The first wedding cake I produced I put on a stand in the shop window in Ponsonby. Trade picked up, I was kept going, and I was able to pay the eighty-six dollars a month rent. I could pay the bills and my shop assistant's wages, and I was reasonably happy. I thought that if I could get a few big orders each week for hotel receptions, weddings and so forth I would be contented. I soon got a few orders that I have never forgotten.

A tall young black man with bushy hair entered my shop early one autumn evening. It was towards the end of February. I had had a rather quiet day, and I was about to close the shop early and go for a swim. 'Cake in window is for sale, yah?' I felt lucky at last. 'Yes, of course,' I said, 'but it's only for display.' 'So I can have cake to eat in window, yes?' 'No, no,' I said. I had to explain that the cake was on display so that people would know I made wedding cakes. He came very close to me. I got worried as he raised his voice. 'I must have cake for me as I get married to Tonga girl very soon. Got good need for cake for chief's woman. She would like big cake for big family. Cake in window will do.' I decided to sell the cake. But he was shocked when I asked him for thirty-six dollars, and began to shout. I eased the situation by telling him he could pay me six dollars per week for six weeks. He was happy.

He decided to leave the cake until just before the wedding day. It was now paid for in full. When the day arrived, he didn't show up. A few days later I closed up early, as the weather was stifling hot. He entered as I was about to have a shower. I had left the shutter half way down, as I was expecting Dave's sister, Jennifer, to call for me. As I hurried from the shower the big Tongan chap shouted, 'No need for cake. No longer got woman. She fled to the islands. No more wedding.' 'You think you've got a problem?' I said. 'Bloody hell, man, I got no woman either. Anyone I get I can't keep for myself. I seem to mess it up. I can't seem to please them. I'm no good, no damn good.' He raised his voice. 'Me no good. My woman no better. So she goes off with big chief. No more need for cake. Got no woman.'

That's no surprise, I thought, and wondered who the hell would want to marry him in any case. I made a joke out of it. 'Well, sure there's no harm done. You'll soon find another who'll be glad to share your cake with you. Plenty of apples in the orchard.' He growled, 'You white arse, no six dollars now. You have cake. Keep it or eat it, man.' I decided to act tough and very businesslike. 'Sorry, mate,' I said. 'You ordered the cake, paid for it. I'm closed.' I sighed with relief as he made his way out.

I took the chance and walked away. I took off my shorts, stepped into the shower, and began to feel somewhat relieved and refreshed. I had stood by my principles ... Suddenly I heard something in the kitchen and shouted, 'Is that you, Jennifer?' I decided to peep out, only to come face to face with the tall islander.

I ran from the shower. I knew what to expect now. I was sure I heard the shutters go up, and was glad to see Jennifer. I shouted to her to hurry to Tony's and tell him I was in real trouble. I prayed she'd fly. Tony's was only two shops away. He was a young butcher from Yugoslavia and had become an instant friend of mine.

Tony wasted no time in coming to my aid. I was struggling fiercely on the floor of the kitchen when he pulled the chap off me. I had suffered a few punches and minor cuts, but I was glad to see Tony chase the man from the shop.

A few days later I got a call from Pa-Joe at six o'clock in the evening. I was asked to go to Frank Quinn's shop to help defuse what looked like becoming a nasty situation. When I got there I was amazed to see a big crowd of islanders around the shop. Then I came face to face with the tall man from Tonga. He shouted at me, 'You got cake. I need my woman's money.' The police came. I was quickly informed that the man was a known trouble-maker, and I was told to get a solicitor's letter sent to him, quickly, about the law of harassment. Thanks to Pa-Joe, this was speedily done.

I WAS INVITED to supply sponge cakes and boxes of canned fruit and pastries for a wedding in Helensville, near Auckland. I was pleased about this order, as my business was struggling. I was duly invited to the wedding and advised to bring a partner. I invited a young woman whom I met at a church social that was held each Sunday in the parochial hall after Mass. Maria was delighted to accept. Once again I had fallen instantly in love with her undeniable beauty.

Maria was a tall, attractive blonde. Her long hair was often tied up in a bun, and this helped to make her somewhat cross-looking. Her blue eyes seemed to send out signals; again I got it wrong. She was, like most of the New Zealand girls, a very independent young woman. I was taken by surprise when on one occasion she brought along her ten-year-old daughter.

I was anxious that Maria would not be late calling, as it was to be one of the biggest weddings the city had seen. A German businessman was marrying the daughter of a wealthy Maori businessman. I made a bad choice in bringing Maria.

I was keen to be on time, but Maria was late calling for me at the shop. She wasn't a bit perturbed; in fact she began to make herself up some more. She was so long in the bathroom that by the time we got going I was thinking it would be better if we didn't go at all. I had been warned by Dave earlier that the Maoris never liked people who chose to be late for their special occasions. They thought it a very bad sign, and so did I.

When we walked into the function room, everyone was seated at the dining tables ready to eat. The wedding service was over. All eyes were on us as we walked across the floor to take our seats. I knew Maria was not enjoying the meal. Then she excused herself to go to the women's room, and didn't return.

A few nights later Maria let herself in. I was alone having a nap; suddenly I got a whiff of her beautiful fragrance. I knew she was close, but not that close. I was instantly overwhelmed by her nakedness. The moment her body closed in on mine, it was too much. I could never hold back long enough to fulfil her needs. 'Is that it, Larry?' I felt relieved, but awful that I couldn't please her.

I soon learnt that going out on a date with a New Zealand girl gave me no right of ownership—not even for that few hours. I was never too sure whether I had a girl or not, even when I had paid in to a night spot or to a dance. The words that stuck in my mind now whenever I dated a local girl were the words I heard from the young male customers who came into my shop each morning on their way to work. They were mostly English lads in their mid-twenties or early thirties. 'Never marry a Kiwi, mate, or you'll end up in our alimony club.' For the first time since I left Dublin I began to be selective in my choice of women.

IT WAS A custom to hold Mass in a parishioner's home one evening a week. I was working in the shop one day when the priest called by to ask me if I would hold a Mass. I felt I had no choice but to agree. He then invited me along to a Mass that evening so that I would learn about the custom and how it operated. 'You can bring along some friends. Sure 'tis a lovely occasion.' Pa-Joe phoned to say he would be there, with Frank and Margaret.

I felt strange sitting in the main room of a Maori businessman's house. Frank and Margaret were seated beside Pa-Joe, Brigid, and myself. A small table was set in the centre with lighted candles and a crucifix. The priest began with a prayer, then questions on our religion and a talk. I wasn't keen on it at all. I didn't like chat show religion or Mass outside of the church.

Because I was new and from Ireland, I had the feeling everyone was watching me. When I was called on to give my opinion to the forty people in the room, I was horrified. I whispered to Pa-Joe, 'Why didn't you tell me?' He couldn't stop laughing, and it got to me as I began to speak. Pa-Joe was a university student and enjoyed himself to the full, often at the expense of others, including myself.

When I began to speak, a dead silence fell over the room. The woman of the house gently placed a full glass of wine before me on the table. It was, I heard from Brigid, the custom to drink it all in thanksgiving. I was still a non-drinker at that time, but I didn't wish to cause any insult. I took up the glass of red wine and downed it. To my horror, it poured down my nose, and I began to cough and choke on it. Pa-Joe

140

was bursting at this stage. I looked down at Brigid and whispered, 'I've got to get out of here—let's go.' The look on her face was one of disbelief; she swiftly informed me that it would be the lowest form of insult to the people if I did. Pa-Joe hissed at me to stay. 'They'd kill us if we tried to go,' he whispered. I took their advice, and decided to speak on religion as I was taught it as a child in Artane Industrial School.

If a pin had dropped, it is possible I would have heard it. When I had finished telling them about Artane and the Christian Brothers, my feeling was that I had revealed too much. I almost felt ashamed to be Irish. But one Maori man came up to me with a wide smile and said, "Scuse me, sir, you Irishman, have no fear, as there are bad ones all over the land. Everywhere you can find bad people. But many more much better also.' He reached out his hand, and I held it as he said, 'You know, man without woman of his own no good. Not man at all. You mention Brothers in Christ who were like priest but flogged little children.' I nodded. 'Well, I believe that because they could not have woman or have many wives, as we do, make them act the way they did. We call it here frustration. It is not normal for men to have no wives.'

A few weeks later I was invited to the home of some other people for a service. After the Mass there were refreshments and music. I had noticed the beautiful young woman with her blonde hair tied up in a bun playing the piano. I was dancing with Brigid when the priest stopped me. 'I want you to meet a lovely young New Zealand lady.' My pulse quickened as I walked across the floor to meet her. When I looked to see where Brigid was, I was shocked to see her with her coat on her arm, ready to leave.

Isabelle was different from anyone I'd dated before. She was an air steward for Air New Zealand, and earned more than many tradesmen who had worked their backs off and done twenty hours' overtime. She had her own apartment and her own car. Later when I was out on dates with her it amused me how she would suddenly walk away and leave me.

She would telephone me the following day to apologise, saying, 'I'm sorry, but I met an old boy-friend and we went to a house party.' I began to see the light. It was the no-nonsense way she spoke, just like all the others, I thought, as though they couldn't give a damn that they could have hurt someone's pride or feelings or even aroused anger by their self-centred ways.

Both Isabelle and Maria had been married, with young daughters. I was finding out slowly about these adorable beauties I was drooling over, having been well advised by my English male customers, who were all paying out alimony to local women for their foolishness. Slowly the penny began to drop. I began to long for home.

I was very tight when it came to parting with my hard-earned money and was very reluctant to spend large sums on women only to see them disappear with the first school chum they came across, so I never tried to take New Zealand or Australian girls seriously.

Isabelle wondered why I couldn't start at ten every morning and just work until five. I wished that too! But most of my customers were gone by eleven. Isabelle gave me the impression she wanted me but not as a baker. Her attraction was her beauty. I was blinded by my eagerness to be with Isabelle and Maria, whereby I lost out when it came to being with the less flashy girls like Brigid, who had more of my ways than I realised. But I never let Brigid get too close for me to find out, though we did date on occasion.

I was delighted I had made friends that winter with a car repossessor. His name was Peter, and he was from a place near Morrisville, but he lived only a mile from Ponsonby, near the sea. He was a tall chap in his late twenties, married to a beauty from Hamilton, called Lee Anne. She reminded me of my favourite singer, Joan Baez, singing the beautiful 'Ballad of Mary Hamilton'. Peter had a strange job, while I found his wife had strange customs.

I was closing up shop one evening when Peter dropped by. He needed my help with a car he had repossessed earlier.

Peter was always prepared for the worst, and carried a blackjack and a shotgun wherever he went! On this evening I noticed that he was worried about something. 'Can I phone Lee Anne?' 'Sure, go ahead,' I said. As he put the phone down I could hear him quietly swear, 'No fucking reply. Fuck her,' he moaned again.

Although I found I got along better in New Zealand by simply agreeing with people and going along with them, I soon realised I was being far too agreeable.

Peter's house was in a beautiful suburb. As the car slowed down I admired the tree-lined street, each timber house on its own plot, with mature gardens. Peter seemed anxious. 'You go on in, Pat. The back door is open. I'll be in after you, okay? Go on, mate.' I looked back as I headed for the house, and I was astonished to see Peter pull out a shotgun.

I opened the back door quietly and entered. I walked through into the living-room. Straight from the shower walked Lee Anne, with this tall, handsome man I'd never met. 'Good heavens, Pat, how did you get here?' I gasped as Peter walked in and said, 'I brought him.'

I never saw a bloke take flight as quickly as the other man. He brushed past me, holding a bath towel around his bottom, but as he reached the kitchen he dropped it. As I ran out the front door, Lee Anne stood shouting after Peter. 'Please, please don't shoot him, Peter. It's all my fault.'

Then we heard the shots. Lee Anne gripped me hard. I froze. 'I'll go. I've got to stop him.' I ran down the side road, and I could see Peter standing in the middle of the road, with the shotgun in his arms. There was the other chap, standing holding his buttocks. He was terrified. Blood oozed from the birdshot that had punctured his bottom. 'I sprayed the bastard, Pat. I blew the arse off him. He won't touch my wife ever again.'

He surprised me then as he ordered me to follow him. 'I better give him a lift to the doctor, or even drop him at the hospital. The cops could be along any minute, and that would make things worse.' I gave him a hand to lift the chap

143

into the car. 'Where to, mate—home or hospital? You're lucky it's not to the morgue. I know you, mate. I know where you hang out and where you do your drinking. You're Roy Dexter, from the south side.'

As he pulled up at the hospital he said, 'There's an overall in the back of the car. Put it on yah. You best tell them you were out in the woods on a shoot and you got hit by accident.' Peter laughed, then added, 'It was a case of being in the wrong place at the wrong time, mate.' He winked at me and smiled.

On the drive back to his place he was quiet. I asked him to let me out, but it was as though he didn't hear me. I tried to calm him. 'You've got a lovely wife. I'm certain she needs to be loved, and I hope you stay with her.' I followed him into the house.

Suddenly I got a smack on the back. 'She's gone, Paddy. She's gone, mate. There's a note—read it.' He held his two bloodied hands to his face while I read: 'Dear Peter, I am so ashamed of myself and for what happened today. I promise you it won't ever happen again. I doubt you'll want me back. I'm so ashamed to know that your friend saw me as he did. It makes it harder for me in every way. If you need me or love me, I'll be at my Mam's place. Love, Lee Anne.'

Without warning, Peter shouted, 'Here, Pat, I want you to take a drink with me and then tell me what I should do. What would you do, mate?' I felt I had to please him. I took the glass of lager; it helped. 'Well, I'd let the dust settle. Wait a day or two, Peter, then go to her if she hasn't returned. After all, Peter, you shot the fecker's arse off! He had it coming. You won, but don't lose her.' His voice was calm. 'I like you, Pat. I love the Irish, mate. You're honest folk, which makes you special. I wish Lee Anne had a chap like you, Paddy. I mean it.' I wished it too.

I WAS HEAVILY involved in sport as the winter came. Suddenly I began to enjoy going to bed at night, as the climate was much like home now. I joined the GAA club for the forthcoming football and hurling league. I was asked by Peter to join the soccer club he was in, and I obliged. I enjoyed every moment playing alongside Peter. Soccer was at about the same level as any one of the junior leagues at home, but no better. Rugby was the main New Zealand sport. There were only about five or six Gaelic clubs in Auckland, and Celtic were the best of a poor lot.

I helped Celtic to win the cup and the league. We had one away game, which was in Wellington, and we hired a plane to fly us all down. There was a punch-up on board and a mini-riot in the hotel on the eve of the match, and the match itself started with one Celtic player thumping me all over the place. I took quite a few blows from the lad before I hit back, then he gave me a vicious look as he said, 'Let that even it for my brother, John Joe.' I realised then what it was all about. I had punched his brother on the jaw a few weeks before in a fierce tussle. He had swung out of my jersey and I had lashed out. We won the cup, and I had it on show in my shop window.

The winter was wet but mild. I decided to try to sell the lease on the small bakery business, but there were bakeries for sale in every second street. The country was troubled by England joining the EEC, and concerned about their beef, butter, lamb and cheese trade.

I was struck by the many good things in New Zealand, and I realised it far more after I had returned to Ireland for the New Year. Going into Auckland for a bit of shopping was made more comfortable by the practice of having a white line dividing the city footpaths in two. To walk up the main footpaths you had to stay inside on the left-hand or shop window side; people walking down had to remain on the outside of the pavement. It was all very orderly. You could only cross the street with the wardens, who were at special pedestrian crossings; anyone caught crossing through the traffic got an automatic on-the-spot fine. Churchgoers always went into the church rather than standing at the back.

On the whole, people were most orderly, and more tolerant than I had expected.

I noticed as time passed that Irish people stuck closely together and rarely mixed with other nationals, yet I found that I was odd in that sense: I liked to mix with people from foreign lands.

17

A Face from the Past

One afternoon in the spring of 1971 I was cleaning up in the shop. Business had not been good; I suited myself when it was time to close. Just as I was about to finish for the day, a tall, middle-aged man entered the shop. I had the cakes and bread that were left over ready to bring down to the convent. This, I found, was the best way of parting with the leftovers. I was advised by business friends in the area that it was very bad for business to give even stale bread away free. They had a point, but as far as I was concerned, it wouldn't make me any poorer.

'Hello, father. What can I do for you?' He came closer. 'I'm a missionary brother, not a priest.' He smiled. 'I travel Asia in my work for the missions. Most of our members have to do some work on the land every day and teach others the same.'

He looked familiar. From where I was standing he looked like Brother Simon, who came to stay for a few weeks in Marino. We had shared a room together. But could it be him?

'Would you like some tea, Brother?' I plugged in the kettle. As we sat down for tea, I noticed his movements. I was almost certain it was Brother Simon. I decided to test him. 'You must travel a fair bit, sir.'

'Yes, Patrick, I travel a great deal in my line of work—and

I need young, bright, unattached workers like you to join the missions. You'll be well rewarded.' How did he know I was Patrick? A stranger would think I was Laurence, because of the sign over the door. Was he the Angel Face, who had come to Artane for the summer up to the mid-1950s for the holidays? I watched as he lit a cigarette. I had to ask him. 'Were you ever in Artane School on your travels?'

There was silence now. I kept my eyes on him. When he spoke again he had lost much of his self-confidence and dominance. 'Yes, but sure I came from Ireland. I was a Christian Brother. I spent a short term in a place called Letterfrack.' I knocked a cup over on the floor, and moved quickly to clean it up.

Changing the subject smartly, he went into great detail about his present work. I reached to the press on the wall and drew out a bottle of Australian red wine. I poured him a full glass as he carefully lit another cigarette. 'Many thanks,' he said, as he raised the glass to his lips.

I was interested to know how he became a Christian Brother. Tentatively I asked, 'Was it your own choice that you became a Brother?' He appeared surprised by my question, and uneasy at first. 'I came from a large family, Pat, being the third-youngest of five brothers and four sisters. My two eldest brothers are priests. One of them, John, is here in Auckland. My two eldest sisters are nuns. We were promised to the church at an early age. Like a lot of the Brothers, I was sent to a Christian Brothers' boarding school until I was sixteen.' He smiled as he said, 'I had a choice, Patrick.' He paused for a moment and sipped the wine. 'Yes, two choices. Go to the priesthood or the brotherhood.' I laughed heartily. He drew on the cigarette and said, 'My father, who was a tough, no-nonsense County Mayo small farmer, wanted me to go to the Christian Brothers, while my mother, who was gentler and more kind, wished me to join my two elder brothers in the priesthood.'

I waited for him to light another cigarette, then reach for the wine. 'Sure it wasn't a choice at all, damn it. The parish priest was forever coming through our front door. Many's the time he'd look at me and say, "You'll be joining us soon, Simon, I believe, as soon as you're sixteen." You know, it was a stark choice between romancing a stone and milking a pig. I didn't want either of them, and life as a Christian Brother in the nineteen-forties and fifties was for a lot of us pure hell.

'You see, Pat, in rural Ireland in those days, parents were strongly urged to have big families. The church was lording it then. It wasn't unusual for the local priest to order a woman in the confessional to have more children as penance for her sins.' He thumped the table, raising his voice. "Tis true, I tell you: my own mother told me that. The church was forceful in its teachings in those days, I tell you. My two brothers often joked about hearing Mother's confession. I remember one Christmas the family were all around the table for dinner, when my eldest brother, Séamus, jokingly said, "I'll hear your confession now, Ma, since you missed out for Christmas." As quick as a flash my sister Eileen responded to him: "Now, Father Séamus, Mother has enough poor mouths to feed, thanks to your Catholic Church. Don't you think nine children in one family is enough, or would you prefer that Mother goes on giving birth for her penance until she could field a football team?" You see, in those days, son, there was no real choice at all.'

'Was it hard for you and your fellow-Brothers in Artane?'

'At times, yes; but it wasn't just because it was Artane or its harsh military system. Oh, no—on the contrary, the food was the best I'd ever tasted or seen. We were at all times given the best when it came to food; but it was at night I found the difference: the loneliness of the place and how I feared being attacked in a dark corridor. I feared being a failure, and I also had to toe the line. In some ways I knew the life was not for me.

'The system grew on me. I couldn't fail my superiors. I could never have let them down. I also feared the harsh life of a Christian Brother; not being able to marry or get to know girls. I did have sexual feelings, you know.

'From Artane I was despatched off to Letterfrack. If you think Artane was tough, well, then, Letterfrack was hell, me lad. It was my job from the first day to take out those boys who were listed to be punished. Myself and a chap called Damian were on duty for unruly boys. We got them out at six each morning, and their punishment was that they cut and draw turf across the bog for long hours. Any boy who didn't conform had to be flogged. We used buckets of salted cold water to throw over them afterwards. I still lie awake at nights at the sight of the blood from their thighs and buttocks, running down onto the cold stone floor. I got to like flogging the tough boys while they were strapped up. It began to eat into me, and I began to feel like a jailer; but the sexual abuse I couldn't tolerate at all, at all—part of the reason I left the order.

'Letterfrack, Patrick, was like deportation and isolation. It really began to affect me. I was flogging boys' naked bottoms in my sleep. I began to have nightmares. It all changed so suddenly. Perhaps it was for the best, really.'

We stood outside my small bakery shop. It was very hot. We began to walk. 'What became of your friend Damian?' We headed towards the harbour. 'Damian got married soon after he left the order, just as I did. Poor Damian, that dreaded disease TB got him. He had a beautiful wife. I only met her once, and that was at his wedding in Dublin.'

The view of Auckland Bay was breathtaking. 'Do you like what you're doing here in Auckland, Patrick?' It was unexpected. I shrugged my shoulders. He looked me in the eye and said, 'Take this, in case you decide to come and sample our style of life. A month away from the hassle of business with us might work wonders for you.' I glanced at the card; I smiled at the notion of me going to the missions.

He suddenly stood up and, more like an order, said, 'Come on, Patrick, let's take a long stroll and see the great sights of Auckland Harbour.' A good time to ask, I thought. 'Whatever became of your wife?'

'Lorna? Yes, poor girl.' He sighed. 'It was doomed from

the start, I believe. I stayed too long in the order, and my health suffered, you see. I was having constant nightmares and awful dreams of my past. All the floggings. I loved Lorna, a very attractive girl from Foxrock. She couldn't live with me—my strict ways, among other things.' 'Any children?' 'No, no, thank heavens.'

I turned to Simon and said, 'It's like one of the wonders of the world watching the great ships on the horizon as they come and go across the world, bringing people to a new country to start again.' He smiled warmly and with a loud voice he said, 'Well, me lad, I couldn't have put it better meself. You certainly would make a good preacher. You have a way with words.'

Suddenly he started a dreadful bout of coughing. ''Tis the lungs, me boy, like poor Damian ... Will you join us, Pat?' Thoughts of Noreen, Helen and Maria flooded my mind. 'What would I do, Brother? Would I travel a lot?' I smiled at the idea of it.

'Good Lord, no, Pat. Very few of us enjoy that. 'Tis my job to find new recruits.'

'Then where would I be based, and what exactly would my job be?' I liked the idea of teaching, as I was certain that was what he meant when he said I'd make a fine preacher.

'Well, you need a direct answer, I see. You don't beat about the bush. Well, Patrick, I believe you would make a fine shepherd on our large sheep farm, and you could also use your skill as a baker for a few months to begin with, to help clear your mind, and you would attend lectures at night.'

By the time he finished, my mind was on the soft rain of Ireland. The feeling for home and my passion for love was too great. I looked at him, and I could understand why he should never have married Lorna. I smiled at him. How could I tell him I didn't want to mind his sheep? I said, 'It was lovely meeting you again, Brother, but my heart is in Ireland.'

I walked away, knowing I'd never see him again; yet he

was a far happier man than I was, and that bothered me as I travelled down to Wellington for my voyage home. I learnt with great sadness of his death a few years later. Some time after his death, Pa-Joe came to Dublin on a short visit. Pa-Joe wanted me to travel back with him to Auckland, to give it another go, but as things had changed for me by then, I had to refuse. He stood in an unfurnished room in my new home and said, 'When you get married, Pat, bring her out to stay with us in Auckland for your honeymoon.' I promised him I would.

18

The Overlander

On the eighteenth of November I stepped on board the great Italian liner *Angelina Lauro*, with over two thousand other passengers bound for Europe, on a voyage that would take me to Chile, Uruguay, Argentina, Brazil, Portugal, Spain, England, and home to Dublin. There was a terrific feeling on board, and I knew I was going to enjoy it. I chose the *Angelina Lauro* because of the fantastic route.

The first port of call after the Magellan Strait and Tierra del Fuego was Punta Arenas in Chile. It was freezing cold, and the streets were full of deep cracks. I never got to meet any of the ordinary people, but a tour was organised for a party of us to meet a few generals, and I was asked to give them recipes for soda bread and Irish stew.

I was looking forward to Rio de Janeiro. The weather was getting so hot and I had heard so much about the famous Copacabana golden mile that I was ready to plunge into the sea once I set foot on the beach.

I met a few English and Welsh lads, and they had planned to hire a minibus in Rio to see the sights; they invited me to join them. The driver stopped every few miles and asked for more money, and the lads simply emptied their pockets and wallets to coax him to drive on. It was a crazy trip. I was broke from paying the driver at the start, and I felt sorry for the lads who had brought more cash with them to buy presents.

The driver was going to dump us all out when we were about ten miles from Rio. As one of the Welsh lads reckoned, we had paid enough to buy the minibus as it was. When the driver threatened to leave us unless we paid him again, one of the lads lost his temper and punched and kicked the driver to the ground. He shouted at us and threatened to go to the police. The lads gave him a choice: 'Drive us as you were paid to do, or we take over the bus.'

He refused. I took the wheel and shouted, 'Let's hit the road, lads!' and drove back to Rio without further problems.

We stopped in Copacabana for a swim, and couldn't wait to strip off in the bus. The heat was overpowering as I ran out onto the beach. I turned and shouted to the others that it was a high tide. I noticed a very tall lifeguard some yards away. He shouted something, but I couldn't understand him, and didn't know if he was shouting at me or at the girls who just passed me, both of whom were topless.

The beach seemed to dip sharply into the sea. I noticed the English lads standing on the wall. One of them shouted, 'You going in, Paddy, or are yeh scared, matie?' Without any further encouragement I was in, and suddenly I lost my footing, as I could feel no ground beneath me. I began to shout frantically for help, but a wave went over me, and I was certain I was done for. I hadn't time to pray for help or even to think straight. Suddenly a mighty dark wave swept over me, and I was pushed towards the stony beach, trying desperately to cling on to the stones. Then the arms of the lifeguard began clutching at me. I tried to stand up but it was too steep. The lifeguard was only a few feet in front of me as the next wave surged upon us, knocking us both forward. He grabbed hold of my wrist and held on, and pulled me to safety, with the aid of the English lads, who were pulling him.

I stood close to the lifeguard, thanking him. He spoke in Portuguese, and then he shouted at the English lads, who were enjoying a laugh at my expense: 'You English all mad, just like your English friend here.' I laughed.

As I lay in my cabin later that night, my thoughts were not on the drama in the high tide at Copacabana but on the twenty thousand huts on the hillsides overlooking the famous resort city: huts made of tin, wooden boxes and even of cardboard that were homes to the poor people of Rio. I felt ashamed that I couldn't offer any help to any of them, except a smile and my prayers. The faces of the women and the hungry children I have never forgotten. Whenever I think of Rio de Janeiro and the splendid richness that is Copacabana I think of them, and their most famous foot-baller, Pelé.

Next stop was Lisbon. It reminded me of parts of old Dublin, with its cobbled streets and its women hurrying to the church, their lowered heads covered in black lace.

OUR LAST PORT of call was Vigo in Spain. On this occasion I decided to go it alone and see the very attractive Spanish port my way, by foot. I followed the road to the centre of the city, then walked along the dusty road as it turned and twist-ed into the hillside.

I got the smell of bread being baked. I followed the lovely aroma, which brought me along a narrow track up the hill-side, where I stopped by a farmhouse high above the sea. There was a fantastic view of the port and of the liner. The sky was deep blue, and I could see for miles. An old man answered my knock, and I asked for a drink of water. I was led into the oldest bakery I'd ever seen, and handed a full glass of red wine. They all spoke a few words of English. The bread was all made by hand. I showed them that I was a baker; I took up the peel and drew crusty, well-baked bread from an oven that resembled a hole in the wall that led into the mountain.

The wine began to affect me, and as I finished my glass it was quickly filled again. The bakery was part of the farm and vineyard. They made their own wine, a beautiful red fruity wine. When I reappeared outside I was seeing two ships!

I turned to say goodbye and I was offered a further glass,

and the bakers came out to the horseshoe-shaped door and stood smiling at me. I wanted to have a chat with them, and I could see they wished the same. We settled for nods and winks, and I drank a further glass of their red wine.

It was so flaming hot outside I began to wonder how I was going to get back down over the rough terrain. I looked at them, then at my watch and towards the ship. They must have understood me: a horse and cart pulled up, and the men cheered loudly as I got in. I could have cried as I waved goodbye to them. 'Salt of the earth,' I said to myself as I left.

I WAS HOME in Dublin for Christmas 1971. After my usual visit to the O'Gradys for dinner, I went back to one of my old landladies to stay. I quickly found a job in KC Bakers and Confectioners in the north city; and then a funny thing happened to me: I was told I was the manager! When I went and informed the few bakers, they simply roared laughing! Tony explained: 'You see, Paddy, the boss tells every lad he takes on these days the same thing. Soon he'll have a house full of bakery managers!' I got the message.

There was a lot of talk among the lads about joining the union. I kept my mouth shut on this one, as I didn't want to walk into it again. I had a feeling I had made a bad decision in coming back, as I soon realised that some things never changed.

I was standing at the oven with the boss the day the union secretary walked into the KC Bakery. With him was the union president, a man I got to know well when I ended up working alongside him in Johnston, Mooney and O'Brien. I was honoured to have worked alongside such fine men as Paddy Farnon.

The boss spoke softly, like a whisper, as I stood by the oven. 'What's going on, Pat?' I was amazed he didn't know. I got it off my chest quickly. 'The Bakers' Union are here, sir. Tony and the lads are going to join, and if you don't agree with them, they'll leave, sir.'

'The bloody union my arse! Who needs them!' He stood

facing me. 'How many will join, do you know?' After a deep breath—and I felt sure I was going to be out of a job after his next question—I said, 'All the lads, sir; I'm not sure about the girls.' He looked flushed. He spoke softly for a big man, and I liked him. 'They can have their union, they're welcome to it wherever it is, but it won't be in here. Never. I built my business without it.'

I could see his concern. He was apprehensive about change, but though I sympathised with him, in my heart I couldn't agree with him. He asked abruptly: 'Are you with them?' He expected me to say no: not even the lads knew that I would jump at the chance to join. I answered briefly. 'Yes, I'm with them. I always wanted to join, since I left school, sir.'

'Okay, then, get your coat and join them, and good luck.' I went home that evening out of a job, but with the news that I was to report to the Bakers' Union in 46 Gardiner Street, Dublin, at six the following morning.

Peter Flanagan, the secretary of the union, was to me a real father figure. That he had turned me down on the many occasions I had tried to join since I left Artane in 1958 was of no real significance. He quickly pointed out to me and the other lads that we would only be jobbers, but that if we were kept in any one union bakery for two or more years we would then become fully fledged members of the union. I was told then to report to Jack Barret, the foreman in Boland's bakery in Grand Canal Street.

I felt proud but apprehensive as I set off from what was then known as the Hall in Gardiner Street and stepped it out, Artane style, along the city quays.

MY FIRST IMPRESSION of Boland's was that it resembled a railway station. There were tracks and belts all over the place. As far as I could see, almost everything was moving, overhead and on the ground. Even the huge ovens were travelling. I had never seen such plant before, and I was instantly confused by it all. As I was a skilled tablehand-baker, I began to wonder what all the fuss was about that prevented ex-Artaners like myself from setting foot on their sacred union soil. As far as I could see, a pig farmer could do the work just as well as any of those men who served four-year apprenticeships.

I was surrounded by old acquaintances. 'Oh, God,' I moaned as I was put working alongside my first foreman in Bradley's Home Bakery in Fairview, Eddie Kavanagh. For some reason Eddie was known in Boland's as the Virginian. There were a few other ex-Artaners; and soon I came face to face with Mando.

It was an experience to be sent for my first tea break and told to report to Jemser's oven, where the lidded pans were baked off. I got my mug of tea and followed the Virginian over to a table. One man said in a loud voice, 'I don't mean to sound rude or harsh to yeh, just fuckin' tell us where yeh served your time.' Another man shouted, 'Yeah, give us your pedigree, mate. Who'd you serve your time with, shithead?' I looked at the hardened men around the table, and knew I was seated in the wrong place. These men don't like strange faces, or jobbers perhaps. I looked at the Virginian, and he gave me the wink. I was glad to go back and join the chain gang at Jemser's oven.

The Virginian warned me not to tell them too much, and not to take them too seriously, but I felt confused by it all. 'Who's Jemser?' I asked the Virginian; a tough character passing by shouted back at us, 'Jem Kelly, yeh mutton-headed fucker.'

Jemser's oven was down alongside the wall. I looked at the men: tired, overweight, hardened, their working whites worn and tattered and more grey than white. There were five of them, and I was to make up the gang to six, which was called Kelly's chain gang. As Jemser controlled the speed of the huge oven, I followed the gang as we moved in a circle to pick up a long lid from a bin, grab a shape with the pan inside and force the lid onto it, then place the shape on the slow-moving oven. We had to follow in the circle for over one-and-a-half hours, until the shapes were all on the oven.

By the time they were all up it was time for another break, and the lads were glad to get away for a smoke. Once again I was the odd one out, as I didn't smoke. But the tea break gave me time to dwell on my foolishness. It occurred to me that there are more reasons than work alone that make one travel. For some it just doesn't work out. For me, I had it, and held it, only to let it go. I had to learn that when it becomes so hard to find what one is looking for, then it's time to stop looking and start getting on with it.

I was completely disillusioned by the end of my first week with the total lack of skill or craft required to work in the first union bakery I ever set foot in. I was puzzled by the fact that young lads were serving four-year apprenticeships to work in bakeries that were so mechanised that the skill was done away with. Each time I was sent to work on a chain gang, or to stand for two hours in front of the giant travelling ovens loading on pans, I felt I was becoming like them: robots or, worse still, zombies. I never felt or believed I was a trained baker.

The work was tedious. Each day was a strain. It changed me as a person; I became angry and rebellious, and ended up in many a punch-up.

By the end of my first week I had made a few friends. They were decent, honourable men, and there were many like them in Boland's. I arrived in one morning hurrying along, as I was late. The foreman, Jack, didn't like latecomers, and he swore with a vengeance at them. I detested being late, but it happens. Suddenly I heard a voice calling, 'Paddy, wait.' I looked back, and I saw Jimmy Quinn, heavy-built, with a round fat face, but always with a smile for everyone. 'Hold on, Pat. We're both late—let's go and face him together. Be better that way.' I agreed.

He used the phone inside the hut. I watched as the huge vans and trucks made their way in while Jimmy Quinn could be heard pleading and negotiating our way to work. 'Hello, Jack, Jimmy Quinn and Paddy Touher down below. We're a bit late, Jack.' A long pause. I was astonished at this strange custom, and I felt ashamed that I had fallen so low as to be treated this badly. I was a few minutes late because of the train, but Jimmy and I would be late in joining our shift.

When men didn't show up within ten or fifteen minutes of starting time, the foreman would phone the secretary of the union in the Hall, and once men were available they would be sent out for the day, or longer if they were required. All the union bakeries used jobbers from the Hall. Sometimes a man would be half an hour late, only to find a man in his place when he did arrive, because he didn't phone in to say he'd be late. He would miss a day's work.

Before Jimmy put the receiver down I got a blast of Jack's anger. Jimmy looked at me eye and said, 'Come on, Pat, we're able for that crap. We're better than that. Jack's just letting off steam, as usual. His bark is worse than his bite.'

I was ending my first month in Boland's when it occurred to me that I hadn't handled a piece of dough. A record, I thought, for a skilled baker. I was standing with Jim and the Virginian, and I was asked by the foreman what I thought of my first few weeks. I looked him in the eye and said, 'Well, Jack, it's the only bakery I've ever worked in that baked so much and where the bakers touched so little.' I paused a moment then added, 'You know, Jack, I haven't handled a piece of dough yet.'

He smiled. I could see I had touched a nerve. He looked at a man called Mahogany. 'What d'you find so funny? He speaks the truth, yeh mutton-headed fucker.' I felt sorry for such men, who weren't able to find the words or the courage to speak up for themselves and retain their self-respect against such crude men as Jack—and there were many in the trade who were better suited for an army barracks than a bakery.

Jack was a hard character, though beneath his tough style and foremanship there was a man I enjoyed having a chat with about the bad old days, when he had men work the shirts off their backs between the old-fashioned Uniflo ovens.

His voice softened and he said, 'So you want to handle up the dough and feel you're a skilled baker?' I nodded and smiled. I looked at the Virginian and Jimmy; both were amused. Jack suddenly pointed at me. 'Okay, show us what you can do and how fast you can do it. If you can mould up the brown sodas over on Wagger's berth, then maybe I'll have sorted a few buggers out at last.'

The Virginian and Jimmy came with me. The Virginian said, 'For fuck's sake, Paddy, you've walked me into this one! You'll have the union on our backs now. It's a showdown!'

The Wagger was a small, middle-aged Dublin man. He always had a pencil stuck behind his ear and a notebook at the ready; he was forever to be seen taking notes during the day. I began to mould up the sodas. There were now six men around the table. For a while there was silence; then the Wagger shouted, 'Hey, Joxer, I get the feelin' Jack is tryin' to break up the fuckin' berth. What'yeh think?' Joxer was a very short, stocky man. He moved along the table until he was facing me. I worked the only way I knew how. He noticed I was moulding up quite fast, and it annoyed the rest of the men. Jimmy whispered to me, 'Slow it down, Paddy. Take it easy—union men don't work that way. Slow down or there'll be a bleedin' strike!' The Wagger shouted, 'Yeh in a fuckin' race, pal?'

I never heard of such talk, and it shocked me. To hell with the whole lot of them, I thought.

The Joxer looked a rough sort, but it was a false image really. His voice was gruff. 'How'yeh.' I nodded and smiled, but kept busy and kept my eyes down. A messy lump of dough landed in front of Mahogany, splashing Joxer with flour in the face. He stopped work and shouted fiercely, 'Who's the bleedin' smart-arse? Yeh won't stop the bleedin' berth like that.' The Wagger added, 'That's right, yeh won't stop the fuckin' train by throwin' dough at a passenger.' 'You're right there, Wagger,' Jack said, 'There's too many fuckin' passengers on this berth.' After much laughter Jemser said, 'Lookit what yeh started now, Wagger.' I kept working, splitting my sides laughing.

The Joxer got my attention and said, 'What'yeh in for, pal, and how'd yeh get here to us?' I kept my eye down. No response. I noticed that Jack was watching from behind the Joxer. He continued, 'You a jobber or what, or are yeh just passin' by?' The Wagger was quick off the mark. He shouted, 'The fuckin' sooner he passes by the better, Joxer. I feel like I'm on a bloomin' train up here. You know, pal, I haven't moved as fast since I came back off me honeymoon.' The men caved in with laughter. Jimmy Quinn glanced at me and winked. I got the message.

The Wagger kept feeding the men with the scaled pieces of brown sodas to be moulded and tinned up by us. He paused to wipe the sweat from his face, whereupon Jack roared out, 'Too hot for yeh, Wagger, is it? Or is our new friend too fast for yez?' The Wagger's response was fast too. 'Yeh, Jack, I think we'll have to see our shop steward about this one. I get the impression we're on piece work.'

The Joxer was only itching to get a word in. 'Where'yeh from, mate, or what non-union hovel did yeh manage to creep out of?' There was silence now as they all watched me. I knew I had to be careful in my choice of words. Suddenly the Wagger shouted, 'He doesn't bloomin' know, Joxer. He had to feckin' think about it first.' Joxer responded quickly, looking at me. 'I suppose you're goin' to give us a real fuckin' cock and bull story and treat us like Jack does, like eejits.' I decided to tell them and hope for the best.

'I'm just over from New Zealand, lads. I got a job in the KC, and when the union came up we had to leave. So I'm a jobber now. Okay?' For a few seconds there was silence, until the little Wagger shouted down at me, 'All the bloomin' way from where?' The Joxer shouted, 'New Zealand. The other end o' the world, Wagger, to come here to confuse us.' He paused. 'Yeh sure get around, mate. D'yeh mind if I ask yeh how yeh got from down there to here? Enlighten us, will yeh?' I said, 'I'll try. From Wellington I came through the Magellan Strait, to Santa Cruz in Argentina, on to Buenos Aires ...' 'Argentina, bejapers? Yeh come overland, did yeh?' I was about to answer when the Wagger got down from his stand, stood at the table and banged it. 'I've got it. He's the Overlander. That's it, men.' The Wagger and the Joxer stood together, arms around each other, and shouted out, 'Welcome to Boland's, our new friend, the Overlander.'

Jack came across and in his crude way said, 'When you get him noted in your book, Wagger, remember this berth is fucked from now on—broken up. This man can do the work of four men, so from now on you'll have three men with you. Put that in your little black book and remember it.' He laughed as he walked away, rubbing his hands through his white hair. The Wagger was shouting after him. 'You'll remember the Overlander too, Jack, I promise yeh.'

The Joxer spoke quietly to me. 'Yeh know we mean no harm. The Wagger and me just enjoy a bit o' crack, and we know yeh can take it. See y'around, Overlander. And don't go leavin' us now for the Bridge or some kip.' That name was to stick with me for as long as I found a day's work in a union house.

I was prepared for hard work, but hated working long hours on bakery plant, and the monotony of the work affected me so badly that I had to attend the doctor.

I WAS LIVING in digs in Fairview, and it really didn't matter to me who my landlady was as long as I was on Dublin's north side. I grew to love Fairview, Clontarf and Marino, Ballybough and Drumcondra. This was home in my Dublin.

19

The Ballroom of Romance

On the last day of 1971 I made my way to the Crystal Ballroom for the New Year's Eve dance. It was my first visit to a ballroom since I returned from New Zealand in the middle of December. I was hopeful of making a date, and I felt in the mood the moment I entered the ballroom in Anne Street. Playing that night were my favourite showband, Joe Dolan and the Drifters.

The hall was crowded. Girls I danced with were pushed into me, and I could taste their mascara, lipstick and hair spray all in one. I knew I was home.

Once I got among the girls I'd feel smashing. It was their beauty, gaiety and charm that created the atmosphere, along with the chat and the crack. The girls would assemble on one side of the hall, eying the male talent on the opposite side, and they would send their signals out to the lads they would notice watching them. Often the men in their haste stampeded across the floor to make sure they got to the girl of their choice.

I met Mando, and we stood on the balcony judging the form below. I had only one thing on my mind, and that was to get a date or to see some girl home. I looked at my watch and said, 'Damn, I've got less than an hour to make my mark.'

It was great fun asking girls questions as we danced, like

'Do you like the band? Where are you from? Do you like the hall?' and best of all, 'Do you like the floor?' I had a problem in trying to find out exactly where some girls came from. More often than not they would say, 'I'm from the west,' with a total lack of interest, as though they were filling in time. I always got my own back whenever I was asked where I came from by replying, 'I'm from the east!'

Pauline was with two other girls that night as I approached her. I noticed her looking my way, then her smile. The Drifters began to play. I got over towards her friend; she said hello; I smiled at her and then at Pauline. I introduced myself and said, 'I hope you're enjoying the dance.' Pauline introduced me to her sister, Anne, and then her friend, who seemed to enjoy looking at me. Then Anne said, 'If you're going to dance, Pat, you'd better hurry up.' She pointed to Pauline. 'That's Joe Dolan who's singing. She's crazy about him.'

I had every intention of asking her to dance, and now I said my famous piece. 'Would you like this dance, miss?' All I got from her was a smile and a nod.

I was lost among the crowd with Pauline. Then she said, 'You can forget about Anne, Pat, she's spoken for!'

A slow, sexy number was being sung by Joe Dolan. The crowd suddenly stopped dancing for a while to watch their star, as the girls pushed towards the centre of the stage. Many of them were in raptures, screaming for a lock of Joe's hair or to touch his sweaty shirt. I remember looking up to the ceiling and, lo and behold, I realised I was standing right beneath the crytsal ball. It semed to be moving around.

When Joe had stopped singing I looked at Pauline. She smiled. I must be up, I reckoned. I said, 'You know we are beneath the crystal ball.' Her smile said it all. She responded swiftly: 'That's for luck.' My hands were down by my side; I moved my right hand and suddenly it found hers waiting to clutch mine. The MC made a spot announcement: 'Ladies and gentlemen, this spot is two free tickets to next Thursday night's dance, the Ags, dancing to the fabulous Cadets showband and Eileen Reid. The spot goes to the couple standing beneath the crystal ball.' 'Gosh, we're up!' I said, and I thought of her reply to me moments before, 'That's for luck.' And so it was! As I eased my way up with Pauline to collect the two tickets, I whispered to her, 'It's a date. Okay?' I could tell she was easy-going and jolly, and I liked the way she smiled. She never said a lot then, but I knew that girls who said little did a great deal!

It was the start of something that has simply kept going, just as one day follows the next. As far as I could see, Joe Dolan was her favourite singing star; Cliff Richard was next, and I came in close somewhere behind her mother—but I hung in there. It hasn't always been easy. Life on the whole is along those lines: a two up and one down sort of way.

The small car I had bought from my old pal Quickfart was giving me a lot of trouble. I paid only £65 for it, but it was costing me as much every few months I held on to it. I was anxious to meet him and bring it back to him, and I was hopeful he would change it. He had his own back-lane garage in Rathmines, and promised he'd always look after me. When I got to his place his landlord told me he had just moved out some hours before. Poor Quickfart was always on the move—like myself. As I drove home to my digs in Fairview the thought struck me: time to get a place of my own.

I had just moved into new lodgings. Mrs Megan was a widow, a fine Dublin woman. She certainly knew how to put up a good meal to a hungry lodger. She made the best Dublin coddle I ever had served up to me. That evening her words simply swept over me. 'Get your own house, Pat, and find a nice girl to look after it for you. They're building plenty of houses out in Raheny. It's like living in the country, close to the city. You'd be mad not to, Pat. They're going for a song, you know, those houses. It won't always be the case, Pat. If I was young like you again and had a lad like you, I'd push you into one of them.'

Mrs Megan poured out the tea. She was curious. 'Have

you got a date, Pat?' Without looking up from the coddle I answered, 'Yes, I have, and before you ask, she's from Dublin.'

I had to know something before I left. 'Would you mind if I ask you something, ma'am? Could you tell me how you become a house-owner? I'm really interested.'

'I'll tell you on Monday. I'll have a chat with my son over the weekend, Pat. He knows the estate they're building. He's after one himself there.' I left feeling terrific. I could feel the change that was coming, but I realised also that it was up to me to make it happen, and to make the right decision for once!

As I drove into the city to pick up Pauline, so many things crossed my mind. I knew I could have been long since married, but it was I who chickened out because of my job. I never considered that the girl mightn't have minded if I worked all night and slept all day. I was always afraid of the fact that if I married while I had very low wages and was working odd hours, it would never work out, certainly not as I would like it to. I had grandiose ideas of what a wife should be like, but I was apprehensive about making the big decision.

As I PACED up and down the pavement outside McBirney's beside O'Connell Bridge, I was hoping Pauline wouldn't be too late. A baker I worked with in Boland's came by, known to us as Galway. He shouted, 'Give her up, Paddy. She's not comin'!' I was raging that he knew, and I realised when I'd go into work on the Monday morning I'd be in for a fierce slagging over it, as he'd tell the Wagger and the chain gang.

I waited and waited, and still she didn't come. One bus followed another until eventually I said, 'She'd better be on this one. If she's not then I'm off, and that's it.' If she wasn't on this bus then my decision was made for me, as I detested bad time-keeping. I had been standing for over an hour in the cold. I stopped for a last look, anxiously watching the last person who stepped down from the bus. Never again, I swore, would I go through this waiting for a girl. I put my hands into my pockets and walked away. I heard a voice calling me: it was Galway, the baker from the chain gang. 'Still here, Paddy, yeh feckin' eejit. I told yeh an hour ago I wouldn't wait for my bird like that. Come and have a jar and get the feelin' back into yeh.' I felt cold, but I said, 'Sorry, I don't drink.' 'What'yeh mean yeh don't drink. A baker! You're the only baker I know who doesn't drink.'

I began to walk away, and then I heard a voice calling. 'Pat, wait. Pat, Pat, wait for me.' I could see Pauline hurrying, one hand holding down her brown leather cap. Galway spoke to her. 'It's a good job you're not workin' in Boland's, miss, Jack would have your little arse. See yeh, Paddy!'

As I walked across O'Connell Bridge I was thinking that only for that young baker meeting me again so suddenly I would have been off, and who knows where I'd have gone! Back to Pa-Joe and Brigid in Auckland, perhaps.

We used our spot prize won at the Crystal, and as we danced I began teasing her by asking her all the usual questions.

'Do you like Eileen Reid?'

'Yes, do you?'

'Do you like the band? Do you like the Crystal?'

Pauline was quite quick off the mark and responded swiftly, 'Well, do you like the floor, Pat?'

'Yes, I love the floor, and better still, I love those standing on it.' 'Do you mean what you said?'

'Yes, I do; but if you'd behave yourself and turn up on time I'd like you much better.'

She pushed me away from her. 'What! Just who do you think you're talking to? I'm not some girl working in Boland's with that dirty-minded lot, like that baker friend of yours. You don't bring me out to lecture me, even if I was a bit late.'

What have I got here, I wondered! A match, perhaps?

She was a fighter, and would fight her corner. The coolness of the way she would get out of turning up late and coolly dress me down often left me gasping. I lost round one against her style; so I began to drive out to her house and pick her up, which was, I suppose, what she really wanted all the time. I'm a slow learner.

The car was almost as unreliable as Pauline was, but it did the job and it got us around, with a fair amount of pushing and shoving. I began to see Pauline three or four times a week and I was soon calling her Paula. We toured the ball-rooms; she was always keen to go to a dance, more so than to see a picture. Sunday nights were reserved for the cinema, and that was that. Pauline was like any other girl I had gone out with. They all had that one thing in common, which was having things their own way.

My first invitation to her home was for Sunday dinner. It was a nice spring day, and we could go for a drive to Bray, I thought. I wasn't the sort who liked to hang around in a girl's house, often left to admire the wallpaper and pictures that adorned the mantelpiece or on the dresser—pictures of her when she was making her first Holy Communion. I did like company, more so on her family side. I knew that day as I drove across the Liffey that it was no ordinary dinner date, so I had hoped she would like to come with her sister Anne and her brother Jimmy afterwards for a bit of open-air crack.

It helped me that I was used to staying in lodging houses and having all kinds of landladies to drool over me, so when I entered Pauline's home that first Sunday for dinner I really was at ease with everyone. I arrived early. I had met some of her family on different occasions, but only picking her up or leaving her home; I had never sat down with her parents. I had very little experience of the atmosphere that forms a part of family life.

As I sat down at the table with Tony, Jimmy, Anne and Jimmy's girl-friend, Deirdre, I felt strange. Behaving politely was one thing, but being able to communicate in simple terms was quite another. But I got the impression that all was well, though I could feel I was being watched.

The moment I got home Mrs Megan called out, 'How did you get on, Pat?' I said, 'Really smashing—great, so it was.' 'You better buy that house, Pat. She's got you, boy. I bet her mother was all over you.' I smiled. 'Your goose is cooked, boy.'

The TV Club in Harcourt Street was now the rave. I hated it as the girls danced with their girl-friends all night and chewed gum. The ladies' choice was taboo, a thing of the past, and the tie became a relic of the ballroom. The 'neat dress' rule too was soon to bite the dust. I was glad I had found romance beneath the crystal ball.

20

A Home of My Own

I was always apprehensive about owning something new, for fear it would get damaged or stolen. I realised much later it was because as a child I never had much in the way of things such as new toys. Mostly the toys given to us at Christmas were second-hand, or I won them from some other lad in a game of conkers. Whenever I bought something new, be it clothes, shoes, a watch, or perhaps a radio, I took great care of it and had pride in it, as I still do today.

The biggest thing I ever purchased for myself in the first few years after I left school was a new bike, bought in Charlie's of Ballybough for £17 17s 6d. For the first six months I couldn't stop taking care of it, forever polishing it. One day I parked it outside the Catholic Boys' Home for a few minutes; when I came out it was gone. Someone had borrowed it without my knowledge. The first thought that entered my mind was that I should never have bought a new bike: an old one would have done just as well, and no-one would want to steal or borrow it. I made up my mind that once it was returned I'd sell it and buy a second-hand one.

When I moved towards putting down a deposit on the new house in Grangemore, I worried about all sorts of things. What if the roof blew off in a storm, or it was broken into, or it went on fire? It was only after I had paid my money that my worst fears began to be realised—though I couldn't have made a better move, as time proved. I found it a real headache having so many things to take care of that were never my responsibility before, like changing a light bulb, replacing a fuse, a cracked window, blocked gutters and blocked pipes, the upkeep of all interior and exterior painting and decorating, down to doing the garden.

The moment I was handed the key of number 156 Grangemore Estate on that lovely sunny afternoon in June 1972, I felt the weight of the responsibility take precedence over any sense of achievement, and rather than gloat over becoming a member of the home-owners' club, I cast my eyes over the place and said, 'My God, what have I done now!'

I couldn't wait to get up on my bike to get back to collect my gear and say goodbye to my last landlady, the warm-hearted Mrs Megan. 'You'll never make a better move, Pat. May God bless you, son, and look after you. You deserve it.'

I checked again to make certain the cases were tied securely on the back. After a few blasts of the horn from the Honda 50, I glanced at Mrs Megan, out at the gate waving, and then I was gone. I wiped the tears as I turned into Tonelegee Road on the last lap to Raheny.

Within no time I was making my first cup of tea. I had no cooker, just a single gas jet, like the ones we used in the bakery to boil a kettle on. I sat the gas ring into an empty biscuit tin, and connected it to the gas pipe in the kitchen. I spread a tea towel over a couple of cement blocks I rescued from the back garden to use as a table, and sat down on top of another two as a chair.

As I poured the tea I quickly realised there was no milk either. Oh, God, I've got to go out! As I opened the door I noticed my next-door neighbour. 'Oh, you've just moved in. My name's Kathleen. Pleased to meet you, and so soon too.' I introduced myself; then I added neatly, 'Sorry, but I've got to run down to the shops for milk: I'm dying for a cup and and it's made, you see.' Kathleen swiftly dashed inside and before I could say O'Brien's Bridge she was back holding a bottle of milk, a plate of home-made scones, and a cup of sugar. As I tried to take them from her I was afraid she would end up having to come in. Worse luck, I moaned, as she did anyway. 'Oh, goodness, my heavens, you've no furniture!' she cried out, almost dropping the milk. I quickly regained my composure and said, ''Tis coming soon, ma'am'—just like the big picture, I thought.

The first tea set came from Pauline's mother. Each week I would buy one second-hand piece of furniture; each day I dug another bit of the garden. I was feeling sorry for myself one day when to my surprise a van pulled up and my future brother-in-law, Jimmy Brennan, got out to deliver a dining table and four chairs. A terrific feeling came over me with the thought that I was now able to sit at my own table in my own home and have a cup of tea with Pauline, though we were still only engaged.

I was fully aware that I was single and had a big mortgage to pay. I found it difficult at first in trying to adjust. It was like being trapped, and many times I seriously thought about getting out before it was too late. I had often wondered about taking out a mortgage on a house before I actually got married. As I look back now, I realise I had no reason to worry at all. I can certainly smile and say, well, it was the best investment in my life.

By the end of the summer in 1972 I had done much to turn the house into a home, with a lot of help from Pauline's mother and father. I had turned the front garden over a few times. One hot, sultry evening I was using a pick, and the sweat was oozing from every part of me. I swung the pick high and brought it down hard. I was shocked to see it suddenly fly from my grasp into the air, then land safely in the soil.

Just then my future father-in-law walked up the drive with Pauline, followed by Jimmy. He looked at me in amazement. 'What happened? I saw the pick take off.' I looked down at the plastic pipe it had hit. 'Look,' I said. 'Down here, Jim.' He was shocked. He shouted, 'Good God, Pat, you're lucky to be alive. You hit the electric cable.' As we entered the house Jimmy turned to me and said, 'For Christ's sake, Pat, you must have nine lives. You were born lucky.' For a moment I felt I was being drooled over when his father raised his voice and said, ''Tis not luck at all, Jim: sure he's blessed.' He looked at me and added, 'You must have said your prayers this morning.' I was pleased by Pauline's interruption: 'He's fine. You know, Father, he's only a baker. He wouldn't have much time at half four in the mornings to pray. He couldn't think straight at that unholy hour.'

AT LAST THE day of the wedding was set: the tenth of February 1973; and as each week passed a little bit more was done to the house. I had bought some carpets, and when they were put down I was in great humour. I looked around the empty rooms with Pauline and said, 'Isn't it beautiful? Everything matches up just lovely. All we need now, Pauline, is the furniture!' She smiled in her attractive way and said, 'There's much more to life, Pat, than fancy tables and cosy chairs, you know.' I was startled at that, after thinking about all I had done. Although we weren't married, it's not as though we were undecided: far from it.

She had walked out on me on several occasions over my so-called dominant ways, which was the real me. Her mother often remarked how I marched into the house, and through life on the whole, like a soldier. 'You should calm down, Pat, and take it easy, son.'

As the time drew near I began to question whether I should get married at all. I wondered how I could settle down to a home life, and be a father perhaps. I became tense and acted in a rather irritated manner towards Pauline and those I worked with. I was steadily getting used to living alone in my own home, which was bad, as the longer a person lives alone the harder it is to adjust if they get married.

It was a smashing August evening as I ambled in from work to find a letter waiting for me. I rarely received post, and as I opened it I realised it was from Pauline. I could feel the tension mount. I went up to my bedroom to lie down to read it. After the first few lines I felt choked, and by the time I reached its conclusion I was disappointed and confused. Now what is she playing at? So she needs time to think, a few weeks. Well, she can have as long as she wants!

I stood at the window staring out. My mind was flooded with the memory of the many times I was close to getting married only to see it all crumble, for one reason or another, and now again! What had I done to deserve this?

I decided to go for a walk. I stared out across the sea, thinking what a fool I'd been, and as I gazed I got a longing to get on board a liner and go around the world without ever getting off. I decided that Pauline was right to take her time, and that she could have all the time she needed to decide whether she wished to marry me or to simply say goodbye. I knew in my heart I had found a woman worth waiting for. And I made up my mind that if she broke it off, I would set off for distant shores.

My mind was clear now, and I worked my back off on the chain gang in Boland's, stripping the pans with Mahogany, the Virginian and the Kentuckian and greasing the hot bread shapes with someone's old underpants for hours at the back of the oven with the Wagger. Not for the first time did I wonder what kept sane men in a sweathouse like this. It was then I began to realise the meaning of a good education.

In the years since then I find it hard to believe that all the big bakeries I worked long hours in with Peter Doyle, Mando, Eddie and Ken Quinn are gone. Dublin's oldest and best-known family-owned bakeries, whose names were household words—Boland's, Johnston, Mooney and O'Brien's, O'Rourke's, the Manor Bakery, Halligan's, the once-famous DBC, Monument Creameries, Peter Kennedy's, Gateaux, Bewley's—have baked their last harvest pan and crusty batch loaf.

THAT EVENING I travelled home by train. As I walked through Donaghmede Shopping Centre I was stopped by two Christian Brothers whom I instantly recognised from my time in Artane, Brother Crowe and Brother Monaghan. I was surprised to find how young they looked. Both were anxious to know what my opinion was of the system and the education in Artane School. Though I was taken by surprise with their questions, I decided to answer them frankly.

'On the whole I'd say it was an endurance test. As each day began I feared so much, most of all the hard men. It was an experience more than an education.' I tried my best to sum up for them what they were capable of and what they were good at doing. I said, 'Education is not a trial, Brothers. In Artane you were all part of a system. The system came first, and you were past masters at how to make the harsh system work and to make us suffer.'

Their expressions hardened. Brother Monaghan smiled and said, 'Please go on, though I hope you can explain as well what we were good at.'

''Tis a shame the Brothers had to act so cruelly for minor faults. Education is not about how hard or disciplined you are or how you keep order. I believe it is all about learning in easy stages, to help the child's mind to develop. I believe the system you helped to develop only helped to destroy a lot of the good things you were doing; and without those hard leathers in the classrooms I would honestly say that the Christian Brothers would have achieved the highest standards, which you were indeed capable of.'

I glanced at my watch and said, ''Twas nice meeting you again, Brothers.'

As I went to move away Brother Crowe called after me. 'Did we fail you, Pat?'

That was an easy one, I thought. 'No, no, the system left its mark on me, and though it certainly held me back in an educational sense, remember I was a duffer. I also believe that the Brothers were struggling to do their best for us, and there were so many of us. Yet when I left it was a real struggle to come to terms with the emotional aspect of leaving such a strict institution, which I lived under for so long.'

'So what you are saying is that you weren't fully prepared for the outside world.'

'Brother, I couldn't have put it better, though I will say this before I'm off: 'twas a pity you had to be so hard; that was your worst fault. I'd find it hard to fault you apart from that.'

As I went to go on my way Brother Monaghan said, 'Take care, Collie.' Brother Crowe seemed curious and asked, 'What brought you this way?' I smiled and said, 'Well, I've bought a house just up the road there.' 'Ah, well done, boy, a home of your own.'

As I stepped it out swiftly through the crisp autumn leaves I paused to watch young children playing conkers, which brought back emotional memories to my busy mind. But my thoughts quickly changed as I walked home to my own house with its own table and chairs and a bed where I could dream.

As I entered the hall I realised that there was no hearth, no fireplace. A home without a hearth, I thought! I'll have to get a fireplace built, and turn a house into a home.

There was a knock on the door. It's probably Peter Doyle looking for me to give him a crossbar to work in the morning, I thought. I opened the door.

'How're yeh, Larry?'

'Pa-Joe! All the way from Auckland! God, how are you?'

After he got his breath he said, 'Never better. We all miss you, and Brigid sends her love and best to you, hoping you'll return to give us a few laughs in the bakery.'

I was overwhelmed by his sudden appearance. I quickly showed him around; I don't think he was too impressed. Suddenly he said, 'Chuck it, Larry. It's not for you. It'll be the end of you. There'll be no fun here. What do you do if she changes her mind? Jump at it and come back. By the way, your matey bloke who rented your shop chucked it in, said he couldn't get enough to pay the milkman. You did a lot better.'

After a meal together we went for a walk. On our return

to Grange Road we stopped for a rest near the Hole in the Wall, and stared out across the sea.

'Come back to New Zealand, Larry, whether she marries you or not. What do you say?' His smile was rich and sincere, as always. My answer delighted him. 'Yes, I'll be glad to, if Pauline agrees to have the honeymoon over there. Then there's a chance she'll want to stay.'

His eyes lit up. 'Good on yeh, Larry, you're a real pal, and a rare one too.'

21

Love and Marriage

One beautiful autumn evening in 1972 I walked into the hall and saw a letter on the floor. A quick glance told me it was from Pauline. I was invited over to her house for dinner the following Sunday.

I was warmly greeted by Pauline's mother. 'Come in, you're most welcome, son.' Within moments I was being hugged and kissed by Pauline in the narrow hall. By the time Sunday dinner was over I felt I was part of the family.

I could see the change in Pauline. She had made her decision and was keen to go ahead with the wedding, and we began to make the arrangements.

THE TENTH OF February was a clear, crisp Saturday. As I stood on the steps of the church in Marino, I wished all my old Artane pals could see me now: Quickfart, Minnie, Jamjar, the Skunk, Tommo. I took my seat and I whispered to the best man, my good friend Tony Lally from Ballybough, 'Do you think she'll come?' 'Don't worry, Paddy, she'll come, but it might take a while.' I wondered why he thought it was so funny.

Tony suddenly nudged me and whispered, 'By the way, your friends from Boland's bakery are here, and the man who's going to sing.' My baker friend from Boland's pleased the hearts of all the congregation with his beautiful deep baritone voice, with my favourite recessional hymn, while everyone awaited the arrival of the bride.

Lord of all hopefulness, lord of all joy,
Whose trust ever childlike no care could destroy,
Be there at our waking and give us, we pray,
Your bliss in our hearts, Lord, at the break of the day.

He followed this with 'Ave Maria' as the bells rang to announce Pauline's arrival.

After the ceremony we set off from the airport on our honeymoon: two weeks in El Arenal, Spain.

IT TOOK ME a long time to get used to the fact that I was married. I was amazed at the number of difficulties I had to face in the sudden change from being single and being able to please myself about whatever I wanted to do to being a married man and having to learn to share myself and my time and to relate to my wife as my partner.

I was exhausted coming home from Boland's, and became a real mixture of all sorts. I wasn't able to understand Pauline's problems, and there were problems from the day we crossed the threshold in the house in Grangemore estate.

Pauline was pleasant and easy-going, as she is today. Thank goodness for that, as I was so domesticated and dominant. My concept of marriage must have been very different from hers. I believed in the old style: she would be waiting with my dinner cooked, and a smile, as I came in from another hard day at work. But to my amazement I would arrive home to find a note saying, 'Dear Pat, As you could be out all hours and as you yourself don't very well know what time you'll be home at, I'm in Mother's and I will have my dinner.'

Once I got over the shock of her not being at home for the umpteenth time, I'd swear under my breath at the way she would sign off the note with, 'Good luck—you can help yourself. Love, Pauline.' Help myself? I wasn't fit to stand up when I got in after being out from before five in the morning. I'd laugh at the whole idea of her 'take it easy' style and 'don't worry'. This kind of situation in a newly married's home is fun for television viewers, but it's not funny in reality to stare into an empty fridge or to put on the kettle for a cup of tea only to find there's no milk.

After a few weeks I began to realise that there was a lot more to being married than I had imagined. I was soon to come face to face with hurt of a different kind, as I discovered when, on arriving in from work, I might pass some remark more suitable for the chain gang in Boland's than for the sensitive ears of my wife. Even when I'd only mutter or grumble a harsh remark—though it wouldn't seem harsh to me—she would pick it up. Soon I discovered that I couldn't behave as though I was coming home to the lads in the Catholic Boys' Home; and yet as I would hear the door slam I would say to myself, 'Good God, what have I done now? Ah, sure I just said the wrong thing.' I'd laugh at my simple explanation. 'I said the wrong thing—that's all.' I've been saying the wrong thing for years.

I had to accept that Pauline's needs had to come first, even the smallest of those needs: letting her go off to see her mother, and agreeing to go with her at a moment's notice. After trying this for a few months I found it was going to her head, and stuck to my own way, which was to agree with her only when she was right; but that doesn't always work either! Whenever we had a difference of opinion, I seemed to think it was my opinion that counted, without giving much thought to Pauline's. 'You never listen, Pat, to my side,' she'd say, and I would instantly reply, 'But you know I heard you, Pauline; although I'm watching the match, that doesn't mean I haven't heard you.' Pauline's swift reply is still the same: 'You may have heard me, Pat, but you're not listening.'

I believe after all these years of trial and error that she was right in many ways and I was wrong. I was far too domesticated for Pauline: I always had to be doing something or other, like tidying, cleaning the windows, dusting everything, while she was only concerned with watching her favourite programme on television. What surprised me was that she would never thank me for doing a good job in the house or in the garden. I'd march in feeling great and say, 'Thank God that's done.' She'd simply say, 'Good for you, Pat. What do you expect, some kind of payment?'

TEN MONTHS HAD passed when our first child, Paula, was born, in December 1973, one week before our first Christmas together. The experience made a huge change to my marriage; it tied me down and made me a better person. Just one year later we had the best New Year's present we could have hoped for when John Patrick was born, named after my father. While Paula had her baby brother to keep her occupied, Pauline was constantly busy with the two children. Money was tight; every last penny I could earn was needed in the home.

THE SUMMER OF 1975 was one to remember. I was more or less putting up with my lot as a baker, working long hours, getting up before dawn and getting home after dark. I longed to write; but when I came home and sat down to discuss my dreams with Pauline, she would only encourage me to go up to bed and do my dreaming there!

I began to get some encouragement to write about my childhood. While I was in Boland's I had heard the men say whenever Artane School was mentioned that a book should be written on that place. The more I heard it said the more inspired I'd become, only to find myself too tired to think, let alone write.

In August I was out in the front garden. The sun was high, the sky was blue and cloudless, and I was leaning on the wooden fence when I heard a van pull up. A man got out and walked towards me. 'I'm looking for Pat, he's a baker. I think it's Touher or something like that.' I said, 'You've found him. What can I do for you?' He reached out his hand and introduced himself. 'I'm Jimmy Mack. How would you like to come back to work and manage the home bakery for us? We need a good man who knows his job and who's the best at the soda bread.'

I agreed to go down to the bakery in Windsor Avenue in Fairview and talk to the boss. I knew Jim Behan well, as I had worked with him and for him in Bradley's when he took it over. I liked him and his family. I have fond memories of the days I went out to his mother's in Bray to help with the harvest, which brought back memories of my own childhood in Barnacullia.

For the next six years I managed the bakery with the help of Ken Quinn. I was back to what was Mick Bradley's Pure Buttermilk Home Bakery.

I began to enjoy work, as I was at the heart of things in Behan's Home Bakery, back to my roots. I had moved from Grangemore to Woodville estate in Coolock, and whether by luck or by error I discovered I was back in full view of Artane School and that I would be passing it every day of the week. I saw quite a lot of the Macker and his colleagues around the area.

IT WAS ABOUT this time that Ken Quinn talked me into doing a soccer referee's course under Kevin Redmond and Tommy Hand. I was none too keen. Since I was a child I've had a phobia about written tests or exams. At first I dismissed the idea; then I began to see myself out on the pitch among twenty-two players, running with them, enjoying one of the greatest field games in the world. A feeling of warm excitement began to grip me.

'How do I become a ref?'

'Well, Pat, for a start, I believe you'd make a darn good ref. You played the game for years, and you're a strict, no-nonsense sort of person. You'd have to have a hard neck also—you'd have to make some awful decisions, which all referees do at times, and get away with it, and be able to put up with a barrage of abuse after some matches.' No, that's not for me: I couldn't put up with all that dreadful abuse.

After a moment I said, 'It was a fine idea while it lasted.' But the thought still excited me. I was hoping Ken would encourage me some more.

'You chickened out without giving it a real go. It's not like you, Pat. I thought you had more guts. I could really picture you keeping up with the fittest and the best.'

I turned to Ken and said, 'When does the course begin?'

'Tonight at half seven in Kevin Street, and it's all over on Friday, when you sit the exam on the rules of the game. There's no need to worry. You'll learn as you go along.'

I nodded and said, 'Okay, I'll go along and see what happens.'

The referees' course turned out to be a most enjoyable experience. I met people who were just as scared of written tests as I was, but the inspectors and committee members from the Irish Soccer Referees' Society went out of their way to make the course run as smoothly as possible for us all. The chief inspector at that time was Kevin Redmond, and he was my guiding light. His relaxed manner ensured that every one of the class of forty had a comfortable passage through the short course.

The more forceful characters, like Seán Fitzpatrick, Albert Walsh and the driving force behind the Dublin branch of the Referees' Society, Tommy Hand, lectured us constantly on the rules of the game until we were ready to scream 'foul.' It was men like them and, later, the calming influence of big Willy Attley that ensured the course was a success. With their help we became good referees. It was their untiring and devoted work that had brought the Irish Referees' Society to the top. Our soccer refs are now gracing foreign fields all over the world—though I'm contented with my lot out in council pitches: a foreign trip for me on a wet Sunday morning would be to the Bog of the Ring or out to Loughshinny by the sea!

I was given no less than three match cards for the weekend. Kevin Redmond signed the cards for me and said, 'Follow the simple rules, Pat, and you won't go far wrong.

Treat the players as you would wish to be treated if you were a player. Don't be rude to them, or to the team managers. Turn up well before kick-off. Dress neatly, and don't act like a dominant schoolmaster. Simply go out there and enjoy what you're doing.' For fourteen years I have followed Kevin's advice.

I will always remember my first match as a soccer referee. It was out in Collinstown, near Dublin Airport, on a Saturday afternoon. Fenstanton were at home to Whitehall Rangers. Instead of measuring the balls in the dressing-room, I decided to check them on the pitch, as the teams had changed outside because the weather was so hot. I had a piece of string with me that I had measured before I left home; I had a knot tied in each end of it, and from one knot to the other measured twenty-eight inches—just as Kevin Redmond had instructed us on the course. The match ball's circumference could not be more than twenty-eight inches or less than twenty-seven inches.

I felt really important as the manager of Fenstanton came up to me while I was checking the nets. 'How'yeh, ref? Here's the match balls. I suppose you want to check them as well.' For some reason I felt tense as I took the two balls from him. I forced a smile and said, 'Have you filled out the card?' He responded swiftly. 'Yeah. I gave it to the Rangers' manager. Okay, ref? We're ready whenever you are.' As he went to leave he turned, smiled softly, and said, 'Have a good game, ref.' He turned and walked down to his team.

I glanced across to the touch-line and noticed that Pauline and her father, Tony, were in fits of laughter. As I began to measure one of the balls I could hear them laughing even louder and, like a fool, wondered why. Suddenly I heard a shout from one of the Rangers' players: 'Are you all right, ref?' I instantly looked up and responded briefly, 'Sure. Why do you ask?' There was no response. I noticed that the players were having a good laugh, so I began to put my piece of string around the second ball, as I was not happy with the pressure in the first one. 'Tis too soft, I thought. Just as I completed my check I was approached by the Fenstanton manager. He spoke hurriedly, though struggling to remain serious, I thought. 'What's up, ref? Yeh got a problem?' I answered sharply: 'No, not at all. I'm just measuring the balls. I like this one.' I handed him the other one. As he took it some of the players shouted to him, 'What's up, boss?' He shouted, 'Nothing. The ref was just measuring his balls.'

As I drove home after the game, Pauline said, 'You know, Pat, I had tears in my eyes from laughing at some of the comments from the manager and the lads on the touch-line. Though some of the things they said were awful dirty, I couldn't help myself.' Her father said, 'Pat, I never laughed as much in all my life as I did out there. You should be on the stage, I swear to it.'

I wondered what I had done wrong when Tony said, 'If you want a piece of advice, Pat, stop measuring the balls on the pitch, and giving hand signals as though you're a policeman in O'Connell Street directing traffic. I know you've got to follow orders and a rule book, but you must also cop on to yourself and use your head, or you'll be the laughing stock at every match you go out to referee.' Sound advice, and I've never measured the match ball since.

Being a soccer referee keeps me fit and active. I love the sound of my Acme Thunder as I blow it to start another game. Though I am just over fifty now, I enjoy getting out there in all weathers and keeping up with the fittest, and hearing younger players say to me, half breathless, 'How long left, ref?' I'm often abused from the touch-lines by people who blame the ref for every goal that's scored against their team and can never see a great goal unless it's scored by their own side, but that simply goes to prove that no referee can please everyone.

A STRANGE THING happened to us in 1980, when Pauline and I were informed that our children's term in Ardscoil Éanna was to be their last and they would have to move on. It was grand for Paula, as the convent of St John of God was only a hundred yards down Kilmore Road. It was a different story for John: he was placed in St David's National School, so close to Artane that I could feel the shadow of my past. I wanted a change.

I was offered the job of managing the confectionery department in the Old Mill Bakery in Skerries, and I took the opportunity of working at something more creative than making buttermilk soda bread and sneezing my way through the day's work. I had become allergic to baking powder. It affected me constantly: watery eyes, headache, runny nose.

As the depression dealt the trade a death blow from which some never recovered, my first year in the Old Mill was a happy and prosperous one. I liked the style of the mill, with all its old haunting features that reminded me of an old ghost story. As I stood by the broken windows high up in the old loft, the thought occurred to me that if I could only write, this dilapidated old mill would surely inspire me to write a superb thriller! I was certain that my move to live and work by the coast in north County Dublin was the turning-point.

22

Inspired to Write

From the time of my tenth birthday I began to have dreams, visions and nightmares, and they continued for many years after I left Artane School at the age of sixteen. In most of my visions I believed I was being inspired to achieve great things. I was the Croppy Boy, Michael Collins on the run, or Father Murphy of Boolavogue. As each new day began I felt the rebel in my veins bursting to break free, as though trapped behind bars or in chains. But I was just a boy with a tag, a serial number, one of nine hundred in a huge boys' army, where my tears ran cold for years without notice.

I was a dreamer, yet I did honestly believe that I was inspired. Then one day I decided to put it to the test. I was settling down to being a family man. I was happy with myself, my wife and two children. 'Will I, won't I?' I kept asking myself. Finally I searched the house for a pen and a copybook from Paula's schoolbag, and within a few minutes I began.

Pauline shouted, 'I'm home, Pat.' Within seconds I was being hugged by the children, curiously asking, 'What's that you're writing, Dad?' Before I got a chance to answer, John shouted, 'Is it for me, Dad?' I said, 'Yes, son, it's for you, Paula, and Mammy.' 'But will you read it to us, Dad?' Paula pleaded.

Pauline asked, 'Go on and read it, whatever it is. I've other things to do, you know, while you've got time to imagine you can become a writer overnight.' My enthusiasm to recite my first written piece to my own family had almost evaporated, until the children pleaded with me to read. Pauline sat facing me, and as I began I thought, it's so much different since I first recited to a packed dining-room on board the *Shota Rustaveli*. And so I read my new poem, called 'If Where I Lived Was Heaven'.

When I had finished, Pauline had a look of surprise. She smiled and said, 'It's very good, Pat. It would make a nice ballad, you know.' Turning quickly to the children she added, 'You know, your father is full of surprises. The next thing is he'll be writing a book!' No chance of that, I thought.

I was glad to get help from Jackie Dempsey to arrange the music for me while I thought up the tunes. After that my first song was born in the kitchen of our home in Tranquillity Grove, Coolock. Shortly afterwards I wrote another song, called 'Dublin International', to a polka air. Once again Pauline liked it, and suggested I should try to get some money for it.

At that time we were trying to sell our house in Woodville. Business was very bad in the bakery, and Ken and I were putting in only a 24-hour week. I had time to play the songs for Ken. 'Give them to the Wolfe Tones,' he suggested. I promised him I would consider it.

One day, with help from Frank Kelly, a harmonica player, I made a recording of 'Dublin International' and 'If Where I Lived Was Heaven'. I took Pauline's advice and went along to hear the Wolfe Tones perform in the Wexford Inn in Wexford Street. Before the show we were brought into a small room by their manager and lead singer. I switched on the tape, and to our amazement he said, 'Can I have them? I like "Dublin International" the best.' Pauline was quick to ask, 'How much will you give for them?' 'Nothing,' came the swift reply. We looked at each other. Pauline said, 'But that's not fair.' 'Well, you're both welcome to the show; but we never pay for songs we get.' Later I was rather sorry I didn't give the two songs to the Wolfe Tones and be glad they were recorded. Another chance lost.

I BEGAN TO get a yearning for a house near the sea. The winter of 1981/82 was cold, and we had heavy snowfalls. Our family increased in size to three on the birth of our third child, Suzanne Maria. While the baby was doing fine, Pauline was not so good; and then we got an offer for the house. We decided to take it and move to Balbriggan.

As the family settled down in the new house, I believed I had something to prove, partly because I grew up feeling cheated when I was a child. The more I got to like my new surroundings, the more inspired to write I became. It often occurred to me that had I not been sent to Artane I might well have had a better education and a chance to fulfil my aspirations. The fact that I survived the awful experience in London as a very gullible teenager was also by sheer chance. What a difference a little sex education would have made!

As time eased by I began to believe I could make an effort to write a book. The first time I told Pauline, she laughed: she always got great fun out of such talk. I have never forgotten how she answered me then and made fun of my ideas in front of the children. 'Your father, you know, thinks of writing a book. He dreams of such things as being an author. He's only a baker, you know!' But at the back of it all, I was more determined than ever.

I wrote a song called 'Balbriggan by the Sea', and later one called 'The Sack of Balbriggan', which found its way into a Dublin newspaper. I had my hopes up after that. Within the next few years I was sending short scripts and synopses to RTE and the BBC. One day when I returned home from work I was so tired I sat down, steeped my feet in a basin of cold water, and closed my eyes. I was soon disturbed by Pauline. 'Wake up, Pat. There's an important letter for you. Could be to do with your writing on Artane.' I opened the envelope from the BBC, and I felt there was light at the end of the tunnel. I was urged to continue my writing on my childhood in Artane, and I tried to follow the advice they gave me, which was to make sure the story had a beginning, a middle, and an end.

A short while afterwards a letter arrived from RTE. I was advised that I was on the right track and to concentrate on my own true story. I shouted as though in triumph. I could feel it in my veins. No longer was I dreaming of writing a book to sit proudly on bookshelves, along with the great authors of the world: I was writing with a purpose.

As I penned my way through my extraordinary childhood, I began to re-experience much of the harsh details in nightmares and in dreams, only for Pauline to shake me out of it at five in the morning. Sometimes I'd wake up myself to find I was marching and shouting, left, left, left-right-left!

While writing late one night I was surprised to see Pauline standing in the open door watching me. 'It's after two in the morning, Pat. You should give it a rest. You'll be flogging me in your dreams, you know. You were Macker the Smacker last night and the Apeman the other night. The sooner you get it all out of your system, the better.'

I began to write with a purpose, like a man with a mission. I did no research whatever. I set out on my walks with over a dozen refill pads, a bunch of ballpoint pens, and an English dictionary.

Paula came home from college early one day and for the first time showed some interest in what I was doing. 'Hello, Dad,' she said, taking hold of a part of the script. 'I see you've got your tenses all mixed up.' I was shocked. 'What do you mean tenses mixed up?' 'You have, Dad, and it's all through your script. You can't be in the past tense and present tense in the one sentence.' I stared at her as I tried to work out the mistakes. 'Please explain to me.' She was more like a schoolteacher, I thought, as she pointed out the errors. '"Is" is the present tense. "I'm" is present; "I was" is the past tense. You can't have "is", "was", "I'm" and "agrees" together like that. You'd have to write "agreed".'

Then she said, 'You know, Dad, they'll never accept this.

You're not educated enough for such a task. You can't even spell. Even the poor typist will have a headache trying to follow what you've written.' I was sure she had finished, but no. 'If you ask me, I'd say you're wasting your time and expense. Now I need a tenner. I'm going out with Joan and some friends tomorrow night …' I was stunned as I gave her the money. I'd never get this right, I thought, and went out for a walk. I hoped the typist would spot all the errors and at least put the tenses right.

When the typist called with the script, I couldn't wait to see what I'd written. 'Gosh,' I said aloud, 'this is fantastic. I've done all this—imagine that!' I was so fascinated to see my handwritten work typed so neatly that I was certain it would be accepted—that is, until I showed it to Tricia in the local library and asked her to take a look at it. I was confident she would give me her honest opinion. She was indeed forthcoming. I was shocked. It wasn't enough to have a good story; I realised I had to tell it well also.

Paula's swift, sharp lesson regarding the tenses had me very bothered. She was so busy with her studies that I didn't want to get her involved. I decided to go over every page, and to my utter disappointment all my worst fears were realised. It was then I knew that what Paula had tried to explain to me was true. If only she could write it for me!

I decided to rewrite as much as possible until I got it into some kind of shape. I was learning all the time, but I was learning the hard way, as usual.

THE RECESSION BEGAN to affect the hot bread shops that had sprung up all over the country. By 1984 the great progress I had made in building up a busy confectionery department began to crumble. Many well-established bakeries were soon to bite the dust. Even the Old Mill itself did, in a tragic fire, a great loss to the Jenkinsons, who were a hard-working family among the proud people of Skerries.

In the summer of 1989 I was offered a temporary job in the Mater Hospital, as a porter in the Outpatients'

Department. I found myself working with more heart and zeal as I went about the hospital with a renewed faith, and I gained more self-belief with each passing day. I couldn't wait to get home to Balbriggan to sit for a few hours by the cliffs or beside the old lighthouse. Once I would feel contented and comfortable I would write until my wrist ached. Then I'd meander off to John Dempsey's to quench my thirst and browse through the script, only to find I wanted to change most of it again.

The Mater was an institution that brought me right back to my childhood in Artane, with its long polished corridors, high ceilings, and cream-painted walls. What astonished me was the fact that I was still in some way institutionalised. I loved the place. The wages were low, but the job satisfaction made up for its shortcomings. I found it a cheerful place to work in, especially because of the warm and friendly way in which I was treated by the staff.

A call on my bleep from the supervisor in Medical Records turned out to be the door to my past. One May morning I was instructed to take a pile of records over to be stored in number 46 Eccles Street. Mary looked at me and said, 'You know where it is, Patrick? Cross the road opposite the church, and it's down on your right: the blue door, number 46.' She smiled warmly at me, as though she knew that I had been reared as an orphan inside its painted rooms.

I went to collect the key from the department manager. Fionnuala smiled at me as she handed me the key. 'You know where it is?' I nodded and smiled. 'You look pale. Are you all right?' I nodded.

As I stood inside the former home for homeless babies, my heart almost froze. I quickly put away the boxes of charts and stood staring at the rooms, trying to place what was in each room as I had last seen it. I sat down on a dilapidated staircase, rested my head in my hands, and said, 'Lord, what has sent me back this way?'

I wandered through the rooms, their paint peeling from the once brightly coloured walls. I stood on the landing looking down into the wide front hall and smiled as I thought of the noise we made running up and down the stairs as Artane boys out for the Christmas dinner in 1957.

If ever I needed the motivation to complete my story I got it a few minutes later. I went on my break with the thoughts fresh in my mind of the experience I had just had. In the porters' tea room four lads were playing cards. Eddie nudged me. 'Back in the early sixties here, Paddy, it was very hard work, I tell yeh, not like today. The hospital was really spotless. Yeh know, goin' back over twenty years ago here reminds me of Artane Industrial School. Them Brothers were swine: spit and polish, work, sweat, and shine. Should be a book written about that place.'

My heart trembled when another of the card players stood up, tall and erect, like an ex-soldier, I thought. His voice was clear, though there was sadness and anger in it as he said, 'I agree. There definitely should be a book written about Artane. But if it ever should happen, I bet those bastards would climb out of the woodwork to have it censored and to make certain the truth is never told.'

That's it, I thought. I'm going to be the one to do it. I wanted to shout it out: 'I can do it!'

Conclusion

There are times in our lives when we find it difficult to accept the truth, for various reasons. We all have that weakness. In my opinion the Christian Brothers' greatest achievements are often forgotten or simply overlooked. Perhaps it is partly because so many of them could have been more human and kind towards the young boys in their care. Their hallmark was without doubt discipline, and they became feared because of it. The Christian Brothers in my experience in Artane School ruled by fear. Order was easily maintained because of it.

Their own life was not an easy one. The fact that they had to remain celibate was to deprive them of ever being loved and having a true knowledge of love. Why must a man be celibate simply to teach children?

Many of the Christian Brothers I believe had no choice in joining the famed order. Sometimes at sixteen or eighteen years of age they were promised to the order and sent off to a life of celibacy before their young hearts and minds had developed. While most of them were too young to choose that life in the first place, I feel celibacy only hardened and frustrated these young men and made them bitter. They vented their anger on the children in their care, whether it was in the classrooms, at recreation, or in the dormitories. They never controlled their anger, and the children were made to suffer.

It was asking a great deal of these young men to expect them to show love or kindness or to be father figures twenty-four hours a day to the little orphan boys in their care, whose greatest need was for love and affection.

From their homes throughout Ireland young men were promised to the church, just as their sisters were farmed out to the convents to become sisters of Christ and take up a life of celibacy. It was a tradition in rural Ireland that each household supply the religious orders with brothers and sisters in Christ. But the vow of celibacy is the rock that most if not all the religious orders have floundered upon.

The achievements of the Christian Brothers in Artane Industrial School, in keeping it self-sufficient and in giving each boy a trade in a short two year-period, would be regarded as miraculous if it were carried out by a national organisation today. That they achieved so much for so many at so little cost to the state tells us a great deal about them.

I believe that the young Brothers who left the order in their droves since the nineteen-sixties did so to find a new kind of love. Many got married to make their lives more meaningful; with their experience they became national school teachers, and in so doing carried the shadow of their past with them through their new lives, as I have done through mine.